An Illustrated History of the
CORNISH MAIN LINE

An
Illustrated History
of the
CORNISH
MAIN LINE

John Vaughan

OPC

An imprint of
Ian Allan Publishing

First published 2009

ISBN 978 0 86093 625 1

Published by Oxford Publishing Co

an imprint of Ian Allan Publishing Ltd, Hersham, Surrey KT12 4RG. Printed in England by Ian Allan Printing Ltd, Hersham, Surrey KT12 4RG.

Code: 0903/B

Visit the Ian Allan Publishing website at www.ianallanpublishing.com

Front cover: **On a glorious morning in the Glynn Valley east of Bodmin Road, an immaculate InterCity liveried IC125 unit crosses Penadlake Viaduct on its way to London Paddington.** *Author*

Back cover: **The Ancient town of Lostwithiel was once an important transport centre with small commercial vessels bringing incoming and outgoing produce along the once-navigable estuary of the River Fowey. In 1859 the Cornwall Railway arrived, building not only a station to serve the local community but also a major railway works. In October 1869 a freight-only line to Fowey opened, which survives to the present day to transport china clay. On a delightful afternoon in june 1986 a rail-blue Class 47 powers away from the station on the down main line with a rake of empty china clay hoods. The busy sidings are no longer used because fixed-formation block loads are now the order of the day; nor does clay arrive any longer from Moorswater, Marsh Mills or Heathfield, to the east.** *Author*

Half title page: **Climbing away from the attractive town of Lostwithiel in the borough of Restormel on a delightful 22 April 1987 is 16-cylinder Class 50 No 50024 *Vanguard* with the 09.20 Liverpool Lime Street to Penzance. This charming scene features just a small corner of the wonderful topography and scenery to be encountered along the 75-mile route between the River Tamar at Saltash and the stop blocks at Penzance.** *Author*

Title page: **The numerous disused engine houses that litter the Cornish landscape form one of the enduring icons of the Cornish main line. Most of them date back to the mid to late 19th century, the heyday of Cornish mining. The buildings housed mostly steam-powered beam engines, used for either pumping water out of the mines or as whims, lifting men, equipment and minerals to and from the surface. This example, adjacent to the main line, is at Hallenbeagle just east of the site of Scorrier station. The annual weed-killing train is backlit as it sprays the weeds in April 1991, with Class 20s Nos 20904 *Janis* and 20901 *Nancy* providing the motive power.** *Author*

Below: **Although the first 'main line' in Cornwall was the Hayle Railway (HR), which opened to passengers between Hayle and Redruth in 1843, it was the West Cornwall Railway (WCR) that first operated between Truro to Penzance. In this wonderful etching from an 1852 edition of the *Illustrated London News* the first train is seen arriving at Penzance. Of note are the open coaches and the crowds of locals that are celebrating the event. The town (right) and the harbour (left) provide the background.** *Brunel University*

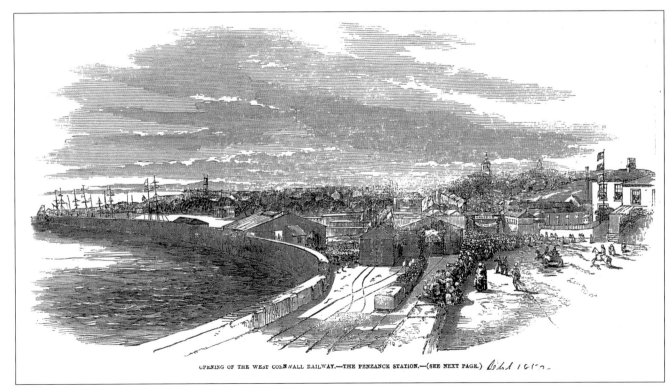

OPENING OF THE WEST CORNWALL RAILWAY.—THE PENZANCE STATION.—(SEE NEXT PAGE.)

Contents

Introduction

The County of Cornwall is a very special place. Located in the far south west of England the county is 'attached' only to the County of Devon. Having said that it is substantially separated from Devon and the rest of the United Kingdom by the River Tamar. In the past it has been referred to as a semi-island but this status is based not just on geography but by language, history and culture. Cornwall is the land of ancient civilisations with strong links to the Celts, which retains its own language, albeit not in common everyday use. Ancient monuments belonging to civilisations that have been lost in the mists of time survive in some numbers, rivalling Stonehenge in terms of their mysterious origins.

The Cornish scenery and topography are also unique in that spectacular cliff scenery, wild and windswept moorland, rolling hills and farmland, small 'chocolate box' ports and the spectacular remains of Cornwall's once world-class mining industry combine to produce an irresistible package that attracts more than five million visitors annually. In addition to the attractions of its distant past there are several vibrant towns that combine historical buildings with modern shopping centres, acres of light industry and even 'out of town' retail centres. This remarkable mix has attracted what amounts to an exodus from the rest of the UK and in the 2001 census Cornwall's population topped the half million mark for the first time.

The coming of the railways to Cornwall made a very significant contribution to the prosperity of the county. Although the railways arrived too late to substantially impact upon the transportation of mined metalliferous ores, trains have conveyed just about every other type of commodity, but particularly china clay and china stone. The railways also 'opened up' the county to the rest of the UK, providing not only much faster journey times but facilitating the mass transportation of holiday-makers, thereby creating an important tourist industry, which accounts for more than 25% of employment opportunities in Cornwall.

The year 2009 sees two particularly significant railway anniversaries in Cornwall. By far and away the most important is the 150th anniversary of the opening of the Royal Albert Bridge and the broad gauge main line of the Cornwall Railway (CR) from Plymouth to Truro. A lesser anniversary is the 200th year since the first rail was laid on the 3ft 6in gauge, horse-operated, Poldice Tramway (also known as the Portreath Tramway) that until 1865 ran from the mines of Poldice, St Day and Scorrier to the small harbour at Portreath. This was the first Cornish railway of any length, although individual mines and pits had minor works tramways long before that date.

The year 1859 is indelible in the mind of the general public and most railway enthusiasts because that date appears in vast letters on the Royal Albert Bridge, along with the name of the engineer 'I. K. Brunel'. However, a student of railways will realise that what was to become the 'main line' west of Truro substantially pre-dates the 1859 CR line, the standard gauge Hayle Railway (HR) from Hayle to Redruth having opened to passengers in 1843, and the West Cornwall Railway (WCR) from Truro to Penzance in 1852 and to its Newham (Truro) terminus in 1855. The two lines linked up at Truro in 1859 but there would be a change of gauge and trains for passengers until 1867. The CR continued with 'its' main line to Falmouth, which opened in 1863. The main line west of Truro had dual gauge running capabilities for freight from 1866.

Over the decades a large number of feeder branch lines opened and in addition, some freight-only lines were also added to the railway map. Some were broad gauge and some standard but the former was abolished on all lines in May 1892. Cornwall's topography called for a large number of railway viaducts to span valleys and inlets. To minimise costs many were built or part-constructed of wood. Between the 1860s and 1930s all of the original CR and many WCR examples needed to be rebuilt, strengthened or replaced by embankments. The viaducts were given classifications by the Cornwall Railway engineer P. J. Margary, Class A for example being viaducts built on stone piers rising to about 34 feet below track level, upon which piers there would be three fans of timber struts supporting the track. There were some deviations in the main line alignment and over time double track replaced single, except on the Royal Albert Bridge.

All of these early railway companies were eventually absorbed by the Great Western Railway (GWR) which exercised complete control over CR, WCR and Cornwall Minerals Railway (CMR) lines for three quarters of a century. Trains became heavier and faster and as the public became more mobile the frequency of trains increased. The zenith in GWR terms was the late 1930s when the motor car was only just becoming established in significant numbers, commercial air travel was in its infancy, the foreign holiday had yet to be invented (other than for the upper classes) and disposable income had not entered the vocabulary of the masses. Freight was booming as a nationwide network of wagonload freight services had become firmly established and almost every station had a goods yard.

The Second World War took a heavy toll on the railways, during which time locomotives, rolling stock, wagons and infrastructure had been allowed to run down, which would have required a major injection of capital to rectify. Accordingly the railways were nationalised in January 1948 and, under the auspices of the British Transport Commission, British Railways was born. Gradually the railways recovered but it would take until the beginning of the 1950s before operations returned to their 1930's levels and some would say they never recovered to GWR standards.

The next major event on the horizon was the Modernisation Plan of the mid-1950s when it was recognised that the age of steam, unfitted trains, manual signalling and a whole lot more, belonged to a past age. The way forward was for greater use to be made of electric and diesel traction, fully braked trains, colour light signalling and a general upgrade in infrastructure. This was to cost millions of pounds that only a government could, realistically, fund. However there was a price to pay and many loss-making aspects of railway operations ranging from thinly used branch and cross-country lines to slow and cumbersome freight operations would all have to be dispensed with. Manpower would also need to be reduced, especially in areas that were capable of modernisation, such as labour-intensive signal boxes, remote country crossing keepers, as well as large numbers of station staff at secondary stations. Trade Unions that unreasonably objected to single manning on the footplates of diesel and electric locomotives also needed to be tackled.

As a result of emerging operational economies in the 1960s a number of Cornish branch lines and several less well-used main line stations were closed and many signalboxes were made redundant. There was an element of rationalisation at every level but from the enthusiasts' point of view the main loss was steam traction, which disappeared from the Duchy of Cornwall in 1962 and entirely in the west country by 1964, when a last commemorative steam-hauled special ran. During the following decades, through the eras of British Rail and then Cornish Railways, further freight line and siding closures took place and a large number of train loads were lost to road transport including milk, coal, agricultural produce and fertiliser, mail and parcels, calcified seaweed, slate dust, light fittings and a whole range of general merchandise. However, on the bright side five passenger branch lines avoided the chop, seven manual and semi-manual signalboxes have survived into the 21st century and millions of tons of china clay are still transported by rail every year.

On the organisational side, the railways of Cornwall have had to deal with centralisation, decentralisation, sectorisation and privatisation with a plethora of train operating companies (TOCs) coming and going as franchises and contracts change hands. The railways have never been so colourful as train liveries are continually changing, not only because of changes from one TOC to another but whenever existing companies have a 'make-over' and create a new marketing or corporate image, with new vinyls rather than buckets of paint being applied to locomotives and stock.

This book sets out to illustrate the myriad of changes that have taken place on the Cornish main line over the years. An immense variety of train types, locomotive classes, rolling stock and railway architecture are featured, ranging from Brunel and the broad gauge with cableless locomotives and four-wheeled coaches to the streamlined air-conditioned Voyagers and the high-tech North American-built diesels on today's railway.

More than 370 photographs spanning 150 years and from an immense variety of sources have been reproduced together with a text that gives an outline history of the Cornish main line and details of the route from the River Tamar to Penzance and Falmouth and very many points in between. As regards Cornish branch lines, a history of them appears in my *Branches and Byways: Cornwall*, published in 2002 by the Oxford Publishing Company, reference ISBN 978 0 86093 566 3.

On a personal level this book commemorates another anniversary, that of my first visit to the Royal Duchy exactly 40 years ago. For more than 35 of those years I have specialised in photographing the railways of Cornwall and for over 30 years I have studied the history of the railways of Cornwall. This volume is my fortieth railway book and my ninth on some aspect of Cornish Railways and to achieve this it has been necessary to read and digest the learned literary efforts of very many authors, spend long periods of time in several centres of learning and research source data and photographs from many major collections. I express my sincere gratitude to all involved in the production of this book in the 'Acknowledgements' below. There is Cornish blood in the author's veins and his, Great, Great Grandmother Eliza Carne, the daughter of the local blacksmith William Carne, was born at Highertown in Truro in 1823 and married to John Born at Kenwyn church on 5 January 1850, before removing to St Lukes, Chelsea, Middlesex.

Finally, I hope you enjoy this visual photographic rail tour through Cornwall, while wallowing in nostalgia at all that has gone before us. Whether it be a grimy westbound 'Hall' class 4-6-0 pounding away from St Austell, a Class 52 droning through the night as it leaves Bodmin Road to climb the Glynn Valley with a heavy up freight, a Class 50 booming across Bolitho Viaduct with an eastbound express or even a semaphore signal crashing 'off' at Liskeard station — enjoy!

John Vaughan
Goring-by-Sea
January 2009

Acknowledgements

With the 150th anniversary of the Cornwall Railway's main line upon us and with the original Hayle Railway's passenger service having commenced over 170 years ago, a modern appraisal of the spectacular Cornish main line has been overdue for some time. It has given me immense pleasure to complete this tome, my ninth book on the railways of Cornwall, and in compiling this illustrated tribute I have been privileged to have had the support of a number of prestigious institutions and able and cooperative individuals, many of whom I regard as close colleagues and friends. I would like to extend my sincere thanks and gratitude to the following, in no particular order: Kim Cooper and her staff at the Cornish Studies Library at Redruth, John Aanonson of Brunel University at Runnymede, Robert Cook and the Royal Institution of Cornwall, Joyce Greenham and the Old Cornwall Society at Newquay, the literary efforts of the late C. R. Clinker, the late John Binding, Alan Bennett, R. A. Cooke, S. C. Jenkins, R. C. Langley and Maurice Dart, the photographic expertise of the late Les Elsey, the late Dick Riley, the late Roy Vincent, Peter Treloar, John Beckett, Peter Gray, Brian Butt, Michael Mensing, Gavin Morrison, Brian Morrison, Sam Felce and all of the photographers who are credited in the captions to the photographs. Also recognised for their input by way of general assistance are the late John Frith, John Hicks, Bill Walker, Steve Chandler, Phil Barnes and Steve Davies. Finally I would like to thank the railwaymen of Cornwall who during the past 40 years have afforded me the privilege and pleasure of signalbox visits, cab rides, photographic opportunities and above all operational information about an immense variety of Cornish railway workings and operations.

Please note that the copyright to the author's monochrome negatives is held by Steve Davies, 51 Eagleswell Road, Llantwit Major, CF61 2UG, to whom all enquiries should be addressed.

Historical Background

At each end of the mighty Royal Albert Bridge across the River Tamar, linking Cornwall with Devon and the rest of the UK, there is the legend 'I. K. BRUNEL – ENGINEER – 1859'. The fact that 150 years after the opening of the bridge and the passing of the first passenger train along the broad gauge single track the fine structure is still in use as the primary rail link to Cornwall is testimony not only to that man's ability but to the various engineers who have since been involved in strengthening and refurbishing the structure. At the start of the 19th century a journey from west Cornwall to London would have taken one week but by 1859 it was possible to reach the capital in less than a single day. The social ramifications of Cornwall being connected to the rest of England would prove to be enormous.

However without spoiling the anniversary party surrounding the magnificent Royal Albert Bridge, it must be emphasised that as presently constituted the Plymouth to Penzance main line was first opened to passengers in the far west of Cornwall, firstly from Hayle to Redruth in 1843 and then from Truro to Penzance in 1852, substantially predating the opening of Brunel's masterpiece.

At the turn of the 19th century Cornwall's mining industry was growing rapidly. Mining for lead ore, which had been practised in Cornwall since Roman times, was soon followed by copper, iron, zinc, arsenic, wolfram and china clay. All of these extractions had to be processed in various ways before being transported to one of the many ports dotted around both the north and south Cornish coastlines for onward shipment. Volumes increased many fold and by the mid-1850s hundreds of thousands of tons were being extracted, transported and shipped every year. Problems arose in two areas, transport and technology.

First, the transportation infrastructure lagged behind the growth of the mining industry and the primitive roads were totally inadequate for the vast number of pack animals and later metal-tyred horse-drawn wagons that were using them. Secondly, as mining became more extensive and mines became deeper to exploit lodes far beneath the ground, steam engines were used increasingly both to pump water out of the mines and

During research for this book the author came across this magnificent and highly detailed sketch from *The Illustrated News of the World* of 25 June 1859, which shows an original CR broad gauge train crossing 'Menheniot Viaduct', generally known as Coldrennick Viaduct, just after opening. The author is not aware that this remarkable view has been republished in the past 150 years. *Author's Collection*

MENENHOIT VIADUCT, ON THE CORNWALL RAILWAY.
(AFTER A SKETCH BY OUR OWN ARTIST.)

A wonderful Cornwall Railway (CR) survivor from the 19th century is this parcels bill for an item being conveyed from Bodmin Road to Truro for the princely sum of sixpence (2½p). The ticket shows a range of addresses in the capital where parcels may be booked, as well as a wide ranging claim that they can also be booked at any station in the country! *Brunel University*

to lift ore, men and materials from greater and greater depths. This resulted in an unprecedented use of coal to fire the boilers to produce the steam to power the engines. Effectively this resulted in loaded animals and wagons travelling in both directions, potentially doubling the problem, especially in wet weather.

The turnpike trusts were slowly improving roads and charging tolls to recover costs and of course to make a profit for the landowners, but progress was slow. Tramways had been used successfully in other parts of the UK and in 1809 the Poldice Tramway from Poldice, St Day and Scorrier to Portreath was under construction. This was followed in 1825 by the Redruth & Chasewater Railway from Redruth and the Gwennap mines to the loading quays at Devoran and in 1829 by the Pentewan Railway from St Austell down to the harbour at Pentewan. The Bodmin & Wadebridge Railway opened in 1834 and was the first standard gauge, passenger carrying railway in Cornwall featuring steam locomotive haulage. After canal proposals had been rejected it was decided that to connect the mining district around Tresavean with the industrial centre and busy port of Hayle a railway line would be commercially viable.

To combat the ever-growing need for good transportation links between the mines and the ports, a Bill was presented to Parliament in 1834 for the construction of the Hayle Railway, which received Royal Assent in June of that year. The proposed railway was to run from the port at Hayle to the large Tresavean mining complex in Gwennap parish and also to Roskear, Wheal Crofty and the Sandhills north and east of Hayle, with an additional branch from Angarrack to Helston. In 1836 another

Act substituted the Helston branch idea with proposed lines to Redruth, via the population centre of Camborne, and to the harbour at Portreath. Good progress was made and via three incline planes the line to Portreath opened at the end of 1837 and to Redruth and Tresavean in mid-1838. The entire 'network' was just over 17 miles in length. The distance from Hayle to Redruth was 9 miles and 44 chains, including the Angarrack and Penponds inclines, and passengers were carried on this route from May 1843, with a journey time of one hour. There were coach connections between Hayle and Penzance and Redruth and Truro, providing a Penzance to Truro public transport service.

By this time there were plans to connect Exeter to Falmouth via a broad gauge line, with the line to Plymouth being worked by the South Devon Railway (SDR) and beyond by the CR. This would relegate Penzance to branch line status, a fact that would have been in the mind of the proposers of the new West Cornwall Railway. It should be mentioned that there were also rival plans afoot, the main one being by the Devon & Cornwall Central Railway for a route westward from Exeter broadly via Launceston, Bodmin and Truro to Falmouth. Parliament considered both schemes but favoured the SDR/CR southerly route. In 1846 the HR had been taken over by the WCR, with the objective of linking Penzance and Truro by rail. In the same year, after much discussion and debate, an amended Bill was passed whereby Penzance and Truro would be connected by rail but with the old HR inclines being avoided. An amended Bill of 1850 had enabled the WCR to lay the track to standard gauge in order to save money but this was conditional on broad gauge track being provided if demanded by a connecting railway. A 4ft 8½in gauge main line from Truro Road to Penzance opened in 1852. To access the centre of Truro an extension to Newham was opened in 1855 and Truro Road was closed. The new WCR line featured one tunnel and nine viaducts. The company ran into financial difficulties and to increase its business performance it looked forward to linking up with the CR at Truro, which it did in May 1859, after extending its line through Highertown Tunnel to meet the broad gauge line. However, for a further eight years a passenger travelling from Plymouth to Penzance would have to change trains and gauges at Truro.

Returning to the CR scene, a meeting had been convened at Redruth in 1843 to encourage the GWR to exert its influence to have the proposed SDR extended into Cornwall and to eventually link up with the WCR. The railway arrived in Exeter in 1844, the same year as the South Devon Railway Act was passed. By 1846 passenger trains were working through to Newton Abbot. Plymouth received its first passenger train in 1848 and the line from Laira to Plymouth Millbay opened on 2 April 1849. The many issues surrounding the adoption of the 'Atmospheric Railway' in Devon and its early failure is not for this book, other than to say that an early proposal for a railway through Cornwall recommended the atmospheric principle and incorporated the use of a train ferry to cross the River Tamar into Cornwall. It should be pointed out that passenger steam ferries across the river were already working successfully following major improvements in 1834. Also this early Cornwall proposal was to have nine tunnels and eight miles of cuttings, as well as sharp curves and steep gradients. The Bill was rejected by the House of Lords.

An amended Bill eliminating the train ferry idea and replacing the river crossing by a bridge at Saltash, where the Tamar narrowed, was passed in August 1846. The main line was to run to Falmouth with the primary branch line being from Glynn Bridge to Bodmin. The line would have easier gradients than originally proposed, generally not exceeding 1 in 59. Part of the capital was to be provided by the Great Western, Bristol &

Exeter and South Devon Railway companies. This trio were to become known as the 'Associated Companies'. Unfortunately, in the wake of what had become 'Railway Mania', much of the required finance was not forthcoming and in 1851 Brunel suggested building the route to a single track specification to save money. Branch lines were eliminated from the immediate plans and of course the viaducts were largely built of wood, thereby saving both time and money. Contracts were awarded and construction work commenced. In some areas much progress was made before the money ran out. In fact the Associated Companies came to the rescue on more than one occasion, guaranteeing the payment of interest to the holders of certain preference shares. Further progress was erratic and an extension was granted for completion of the line. One of the problems with the pace and cost of construction was the large number of viaducts that needed to be built across river valleys and tidal inlets. Slowly the jigsaw took shape, including the Royal Albert Bridge. The last section to be finished was between St Germans and Saltash and on 12 April 1859 a test train worked from Plymouth to Truro. Albert, the Prince Consort, Queen Victoria's husband, formally opened the line on 2 May 1859.

The management of the line was in the hands of the Cornwall Railway (CR), GWR, B&ER and SDR and all were represented on the Board. The Board was keen to complete its main line to Falmouth but again money was in short supply. A further Act in 1861 provided new powers to complete the line and after a further injection of funding the single broad gauge line to Falmouth was finally opened for passengers on 24 August 1863 and for goods a few weeks later.

From 1859 it was possible to travel from London and Plymouth to Penzance by rail, although a change of train and gauge was necessary at Truro. The CR operated broad gauge trains at that time and the WCR 'narrow' (standard) gauge trains. In this view an original WCR notice warns pedestrians at Long Rock to close the gate. *Author's Collection*

In the course of original research at Brunel University during the preparation of this volume, the minute books of the Cornwall Railway were unearthed and, although a slight digression in terms of pure 'nuts and bolts' history, a summary of the contents from the years 1862/3 make interesting reading and show something of the day-to-day problems encountered by railway management.

On 16 May 1862 J. P. Tonkin was appointed Junior Clerk in the accounts office at Plymouth at the rate of five shillings per week for the first month and that he then be 'reported on'. On 11 April 1862 the sum of thirty shillings was paid to Mr Bovey in response to his claim for marble broken between Plymouth and Liskeard. The Guard of the 7.20am down train on 20 September 1862 was fined two shillings and six pence (12½p) and severely reprimanded for falling asleep on the train. The Policeman (signalman in this case) at Bodmin Road be fined one shilling for sending improper telegrams. On 2 October 1863 the Traffic Superintendent reported that the West Cornwall Railway had arranged to run its first down train and its last up train from and to the company's (CR) station at Truro instead of the Newham station of that company (this marked the end of passenger services at Newham). The Post Office had offered the sum of £5,000 per annum for a postal service to be run from Plymouth to Falmouth but the CR informed the Postmaster that £5,500 was the lowest the company could accept. A later offer from the Post Office of £5,150 was also declined. Gas lighting had been ordered for Saltash station on 2 October 1863. On 13 November 1863 the Truro Policeman by the name of Warne was fined one shilling for leaving the engine turntable 'wrongly turned'. It was noted that the 7.20pm down from Plymouth must contain first, second and third class accommodation, the third class fare being computed at 1¼d per mile (a penny farthing).

If fish was carried on the up proposed mail train then it must be charged at twenty shillings per ton more than if carried by the other ordinary trains. On 27 November 1863 Station

Porter Wherry of Penryn station was fined two shillings and six pence for failing to light the station lamps. A Mr Thomas was paid his claim of one pound, four shillings and six pence for breakage of a jar of brandy by the railway. Porter Harrison was to pay an additional five shillings because he caused the breakage. Following the Bucks Head Tunnel derailment Goods Guard Hurd was fined ten shillings for failing to protect the train with red lights. Policeman Lobb of St Austell was demoted to Porter for failing to have the signal lamp lit on the St Austell crossing gates and for having turned on the 'all right' signal when the gates were closed across the line (the crossing was closed in 1931). A serious incident occurred on 29 October 1863 when a van and four trucks on the 3.25am down goods ran away from St Austell to Par. Head Guard Hasson was severely reprimanded but not fined, because of 'his general good character'. He failed to fasten the brake of his van tight upon the wheels. The booking Constable at Lostwithiel was given a pay rise to twenty shillings (£1) per week.

There had been correspondence from Mr Humber and Mr Hull with reference to the proposed Helston & Penryn Junction Railway. Porter Kitt of Liskeard was fined one shilling for being late on duty. Truro Porter Balsam was fined one shilling for setting fire to a partition by the ticket counter. Mr Cross paid the Cornwall Railway £50 for the 'privilege' of advertising at the CR stations for three years, from 1 January 1864. On 24 November 1863 a girl had her foot injured at St Austell by leaving the carriage before the train had stopped. In much later minutes the CR showed great compassion by awarding Caroline Phillips, 'the poor girl who was hurt at St Austell', twenty shillings, the sum to be paid by the Traffic Superintendent. Policeman Julian was fined one shilling for leaving a pair of switches 'wrong' on 19 November 1863. It was decided that no special charge would be made for shunting trucks on the line up from Falmouth Docks to Falmouth station, apart from the rates of carriage of traffic to or from Falmouth station. Also at Falmouth, Mr Wright, the Booking Clerk had reached 20 years of age and he was now to be appointed to the regular establishment at a wage of £60 per annum. Falmouth Policeman Lobb was fined one shilling for neglecting the telegraph.

Also in November 1863 Goods Guard Westaway was fined one shilling for breaking a side lamp. The Traffic Superintendent reported the necessity for a truck weighing machine at Falmouth. The Committee requested the cost of the machine and the cost of installation. A personal letter had been received from Lord Falmouth and others requesting that the down express train may in future call at Grampound Road station. It was resolved that the down express should not be delayed more than is absolutely necessary and that it was not desirable to stop the train at Grampound Road. Also in November 1863 a horse, which was the property of Mr Prideaux, fell from his field into the approach road to the Bodmin Road station and was killed. Mr Prideaux had claimed the sum of ten pounds from the railway. It was resolved that the claim be settled 'on the best terms'. One Charles Rolston of Helston, a passenger booked from Penryn to Perran (later Perranwell) by the 5.45am up train was found dead on the line near Sparnock Tunnel, a train having passed over his legs. The Coroner's verdict was Accidental Death. James Hicks of Lanivet was summoned before the Magistrates at Lostwithiel on 22nd inst. for having on the 11th ult. travelled from Bodmin Road to Lostwithiel without paying his fare. He was fined ten shillings and six pence with nine shillings and six pence costs (£1 in total). On an occasion of a public dinner the Band of the South Devon Militia was conveyed free of charge from Plymouth to Truro and back. Booking Constable Macoskrie of Grampound Road asked if materials for the house he wanted to build could be carried by

Cornwall is famous for its viaducts and between the River Tamar and Penzance and between Truro and Falmouth there were, in total, over 40 structures of significance. The scale of some of the viaducts is impressive, such as the 151ft St Pinnock Viaduct, the highest in Cornwall, seen here. Note the Gothic apertures and the upper extension, completed in 1882, when the timber tops on each pier were replaced by iron girders. The viaduct is still in use today. *Author*

the railway in full truck loads at one old penny per ton per mile (in other words at a cheap rate!). This small sample from the company minutes shows a remarkable diversity of everyday activities occurring on the Cornwall Railway, which in retrospect is a window on the social scene in mid-Victorian times!

The broad gauge CR main line joined the WCR standard gauge line at Truro, where all passengers and goods had to be transferred or transshipped from one train to another if travelling to or from the Penzance line. The Falmouth line and the Penzance line ran side by side through Highertown Tunnel west of the station and the CR Falmouth line crossed the original WCR route to Newham just south of Penwithers Junction. By 1864 the CR considered it was losing revenue by the non-compatibility of the CR and WCR gauges and so it invoked the clause in the original Act that stipulated the WCR was obliged to provide dual gauge track if so required by an adjoining railway company. The WCR was in no financial position to honour such an undertaking and as a result the Associated Companies took over the operation and maintenance of the WCR in 1865, completely taking over the line by lease from 1 January 1866.

Laying the third rail to provide the broad gauge was far from straightforward and significant engineering work needed to be undertaken. Nevertheless by November 1866 broad gauge goods trains were traversing the WCR route, with passenger trains operating in the following March. This afforded passengers the opportunity of travelling in through carriages from Paddington to Penzance. By 1875 the finances of the WCR operation were in a parlous state and yet again the Associated Companies came to the rescue, however all of this was overshadowed when in 1876 the constituent companies formally amalgamated, effectively giving the GWR control of the line. In the meantime problems were being experienced with some of the original viaducts and a rebuilding programme had been instigated, with a substantial call on the company's capital. The relationship between the GWR and the CR was less than harmonious, especially when the GWR failed to agree with the CR proposal in 1881 that the GWR should buy the CR outright.

In the meantime the last broad gauge branch line in Cornwall, to St Ives, had been opened in 1877 and in 1887 standard gauge branch lines to Bodmin and Helston were opened. Finally in June 1889 the CR was amalgamated with the GWR by virtue of a Bill of Amalgamation. By this time many of the timber and timber-topped viaducts were in need of

replacement. They had been built 'on the cheap' at a low capital cost but expenditure on maintenance was high. There were already murmurs in the GWR camp that the broad gauge was doomed and many of the Cornish viaducts were rebuilt to take double standard gauge track. In May 1892 one of the most amazing feats of railway engineering took place, when over a weekend the entire route from Exeter to Truro(see p.21) including relevant branch lines (and other 'up country' route miles) was converted from broad gauge to standard gauge. Between daybreak on Saturday, 21 May and 4am on Monday, 23 May a total of 177 route miles of track were converted by a massive workforce of 4,200 staff. The GWR made progress quickly and by the following year the first through train from London to Penzance featuring corridor coaches, steam heating and gas lighting was in operation. In 1896, the GWR absorbed the Cornwall Minerals Railway, the larger company having operated the CMR lines since 1877.

There followed a period of rapid rail traffic expansion as populations increased and social travelling habits began to change. For example, by the turn of the century, Saltash was

the beneficiary of a frequent suburban train service from Plymouth, especially after steam railmotors were introduced from 1904. Two years earlier the Travelling Post Office made its début. Also in 1904 a demonstration train had run from Paddington to Penzance in 6 hours and 47 minutes, a remarkable achievement at that time, especially via Bristol! Named trains started to appear such as the 'Cornishman' and later the 'Cornish Riviera Express'. Tourism was beginning to develop in the west country and from 1906 through trains not only served Falmouth and Penzance but also Newquay, particularly in the summer months. A further improvement in journey times followed the opening of the Westbury cut-off in 1906, reducing journeys to the Capital by 20½ miles.

Above: **An important location in the history of the Cornish main line is the site of the original 1838 HR Redruth terminus. Opened for goods in 1838 and passengers in 1843, it was in use only until 1852 for passengers but it survived until 1967 for sundry goods traffic, latterly domestic coal. In this wonderful view from 1937 the old station on the left survived along with a substantial goods shed on the right, with a 'GW' wagon in attendance.** *Brunel University*

Right: **In this rather sad photograph from the early days of British Railways the old original HR Redruth terminus, with its fine all-over roof, has been demolished and the granite goods shed is looking dilapidated. Only a couple of domestic coal wagons provide life to the scene, with the local merchant positioning his scales by the opening aperture of the wagon. The site was consigned to railway history in 1967.** *Cornish Studies Library*

This fascinating 1920s view shows Redruth Junction, just to the west of the present Redruth station. The main line here was converted to double track in 1894, with the original HR lines diverging to the original Redruth terminus, left, and the freight line to Tresavean mine via a 1 in 15 incline, right. The 17-lever signalbox seen here was constructed in 1894 and closed in October 1966. *Author's Collection*

The limited capacity of the substantially single track in Cornwall had been realised in Victorian times and gradually the entire Plymouth to Penzance main line was doubled, with the exception of the Royal Albert Bridge. Most of the conversion work took place in the 1890s but it would be 1930 before the last section was completed. Over the decades the original 'main line' route from Truro to Falmouth increasingly adopted a branch line identity and this line was never doubled, its capacity being determined by station passing loops.

In the early years of the 20th century the GWR went into overdrive as locomotives became larger and more powerful, coaching stock was significantly improved, facilities for passengers increased and timetables revealed an increasingly frequent train service on most lines. Journey times tumbled and, combined with growing affluence and greater social and business mobility, the GWR in Cornwall prospered. There was massive inward investment in infrastructure and one particularly important development, albeit away from the main line, was the GWR's investment in Fowey Docks.

In both 1896 and 1923 large sums of money were invested in building five new jetties, which greatly increased handling capacity in the export of china clay and china stone. Early CR/WCR/CMR signal boxes were replaced by standard GWR examples, many new station buildings were erected and new freight and locomotive depots were established at various locations along the main line, as detailed in the following chapters. Completely new railway lines were constructed such as the Chacewater to Newquay line in 1903/5 and the Bojea china clay line in 1920. Other lines were extended, such as the Retew branch in china clay country in 1912. Many new minor stations and halts were opened to optimise passenger train loadings.

Between the two World Wars the GWR continued to develop the railways of Cornwall. In the mid-1920s freight services were greatly improved and fast fitted trains ran non-stop for longer distances at higher speeds. In 1927 new six-wheeled 3,000 gallon milk wagons were introduced. Passenger service frequency was improved in 1927 and again in 1929, before the Great Depression took hold. However by the mid-1930s traffic levels were restored, indeed holiday traffic was booming. In 1935, the GWR's centenary year, new rolling stock was introduced on the 'Cornish Riviera Limited'. Many express passenger trains contained individual coaches or portions for

locations on branch lines. For the holiday-makers inducements to travel were marketed, such as runabout tickets. The Holidays with Pay Act of 1938 produced mandatory annual holiday entitlements and this fundamental social change could do nothing but increase the numbers taking the train to their chosen vacation resort. However the clouds of an impending World War were gathering and for six years the GWR, in common with other railway companies, was gradually run down as maintenance was restricted to safety issues and severe restrictions were imposed on civilian rail travel.

The railways were nationalised in 1948 and as an independent business entity the GWR was no more. However, to the casual observer the advent of British Railways (BR) resulted in little change initially because the Western Region (WR) continued to operate with GWR locomotives, rolling stock and infrastructure. With the available resources BR tried to re-establish former GWR standards but by the early 1950s much of the equipment had worn out. There was a strong resurgence in the mid-1950s when traffic levels began to approach the late-1930s level, especially during the summer months when the great British public took their annual holidays. Under the control of the British Transport Commission (BTC) it became clear that a national Modernisation Plan was needed and in 1955 huge government expenditure was authorised. In most of Cornwall these changes were imperceptible until the advent of dieselisation in 1958, a process completed in about four years.

By the beginning of the 1960s competition with the railways was growing and private car ownership was increasing rapidly. Bus services with their door-to-door capability were free from wartime restrictions and the advent of foreign package holidays featuring jet plane travel were taking potential passengers to distant locations. Many branch lines and minor stations were undoubtedly on the debit side of any profit and loss balance sheet and major reviews were instigated to test financial viability. The infamous Dr Beeching and his 1963 report, 'The Reshaping of Britain's Railways', will forever be associated with this era. Consequently, in the 1960s a number of Cornish main line stations closed, as well as a number of branch lines. On the main line Doublebois, Grampound Road, Scorrier, Carn Brea, Gwinear Road and Marazion all closed. Freight traffic was in terminal decline and while china clay traffic remained buoyant

The HR was taken over by the WCR and it embarked on a scheme to link Truro with Penzance by rail, avoiding the inclines on the old HR route. At Truro the WCR established its Truro Road station in 1852, located on the west side of Highertown, some way from the city centre. Accordingly the company set about extending its line to a new terminus at Newham, just south of Truro.
This view shows the modest wooden structure with a freight shed beyond and an all-over platform roof on the right.
Brunel University

general goods traffic slowly dwindled to a trickle, with many minor goods yards closing. By the mid-1960s certain service train schedules were trimmed, producing record journey times between London and Penzance featuring diesel power. Partial colour light signalling was introduced in some areas and, across St Pinnock and Largin viaducts, the main line was singled to avoid substantial strengthening costs. In later years the main line from Marazion to a point just short of the Penzance terminus was also singled.

Diesel locomotives became more powerful and air-conditioned rolling stock was introduced during the 1970s. By the end of that decade IC125 High Speed Train units started to work prestigious named trains before replacing diesel locomotives on the majority of London trains from May 1980. Journey times between the capital and 'the blocks' at Penzance were slashed to about five hours for the quickest trains. Eventually the fixed formation units took over cross-country services and a new generation of units replaced the old diesel mechanical examples. During 1976 the original CR station buildings at Lostwithiel were swept away, followed by the old broad gauge goods shed. During the 1980s more semaphore signals were felled and their associated signal boxes were closed, such as Bodmin Road, Largin and Burngullow. Detailed changes are mentioned in the general text but many other modifications took place during the BR years, such as the lengthening of the up platform at Liskeard, the replacement of

the station buildings at Bodmin Road (by then renamed Bodmin Parkway), the abolition of the island platform through line at Truro and the building of a new train depot at Ponsandane. St Austell goods yard was closed and the (by then) freight-only line to Bodmin General and Wenford Bridge was axed.

During the mid-1980s the main line between Burngullow and Probus was inexplicably singled, a lesson BR failed to learn from its disastrous singling of sections of the Southern main line between Exeter and Salisbury. At huge expense the track was redoubled in 2004. Gradually all milk traffic, coal, general goods, flowers, agricultural produce and fertiliser, post and parcels, beer, calcified seaweed and many other trainloads were lost, leaving just china clay, oil (for the railway's own use), scrap metal and a modicum of mineral traffic left to represent Cornwall's once busy freight business. Examples of track rationalisation are detailed in the general text but there was considerable rationalisation from Saltash to Penzance.

During the past 20 years the organisation of the railways has produced many changes in Cornwall, with the main visible alterations being station signs and train liveries. After a short period of area delegation during 1985/6, when most of the rail operations were conducted under the auspices of 'Cornwall Railways', the BR organisation was divided into a number of business sectors, such as InterCity, Regional Railways, Railfreight, Network SouthEast and ScotRail. There was a political agenda to privatise the railways and by 1987 the Railfreight organisation was divided into financially accountable 'sectors'. By 1994 three 'shadow' freight businesses were created, Transrail, Mainline and Loadhaul, with a view to sale to private companies. On the passenger front Train Operating Companies (TOCs) competed for various area franchises and much of the stock was leased out by Rolling Stock Companies (ROSCOs). The general infrastructure was cared for by Railtrack and later Network Rail, all resulting in an unbelievably complex and segregated structure compared with the good old days of British Railways.

Although a highly detailed and technical study of motive power and rolling stock that has worked over Cornwall's main line for over 150 years is not for this book, an overview giving some indication of the dramatic changes that have occurred since the mid-19th century is essential. Records such as they are suggest that the earliest locomotives used on the HR from 1837 were supplied by the contractor J Chanter. They carried attractive names such as *Coryndon*, *Cornubia*, *Carn Brea*, *Chanter* and *Pendarve*. These were primitive machines but of particular interest was *Cornubia* that was built for the HR at the local Copperhouse Foundry and was said to be a fine machine capable of attaining speeds of 40mph. By the time the WCR had taken over HR lines and started its passenger service between Penzance and Redruth, the original engines were almost life-expired and most had been withdrawn by 1853. Two 0-4-2 tank engines were procured, the parts of which arrived from Stothert & Slaughter of Bristol via the harbour at Hayle for assembly at the WCR Carn Brea Works. The locomotives were called *Penzance* and *Camborne*. Between 1851 and 1865 the WCR operated 13 different locomotives mostly built by R. Stephenson & Co and the aforementioned Stothert & Slaughter and overall there was a mix of 2-4-0, 0-4-2 and 0-6-0 tender engines and 0-4-2 tanks. Five of these were allocated to freight duties. The Associated Companies inherited 11 standard gauge WCR locomotives upon take-over in 1866. Some new locomotives were procured, and by 1876, when the GWR took over operations, only two of the eight serviceable locomotives absorbed by the larger company dated back to WCR days, these being the 2-4-0s Falmouth and St Ives.

For the CR's broad gauge operations, prior to the opening of the main line from Plymouth and Saltash to Truro in 1859, the Directors had estimated that eight passenger and two goods locomotives would be required initially. The GWR was approached to determine whether it would provide the CR motive power. Although it arranged for a single 'loaner' engine to be used during construction of the line it declined the full proposal and so Evans & Co, the locomotive supplier to the SDR, was invited to also supply the CR motive power. Agreement was reached and a seven-year contract was drawn up and upon expiry thereof the CR was to purchase the locomotives. Accordingly eight new locomotives were supplied. The contract was loaded with conditions and stipulations and a complex scale of charges based on mileage and train load was drawn up. The locomotives were 4-4-0 saddle tanks broadly based on a Gooch 4-4-0ST design of 1849. The goods engine was and 0-6-0ST version of the passenger engines. By 1863 the CR fleet had grown to 13 engines. In 1866 both the SDR and the CR (and by implication the WCR) decided to end their contract with Evans & Co and they purchased the locomotives at valuation, worth £131,000 in net terms after an allowance being made for old WCR locomotives. Technically the SDR then supplied the CR with locomotives. By 1874 a total of 21 broad gauge locomotives were allocated to CR duties (12 x 4-4-0STs and 9 x 0-6-0STs), increasing to 27 by 1884. The GWR

Right: **The little terminus at Newham was used by passenger trains only between opening in April 1855 and September 1863, with most WCR trains using the CR station from May 1859.** *Bradshaw's* **of 1861 shows only the first train of the day out and last train of the day back using the WCR's Newham station. In this August 1956 view the single platform station looks to be in remarkably good condition considering no passenger had used the station for 93 years!** *Hugh Davies*

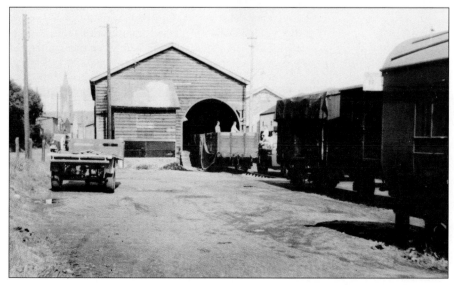

Left: **This interesting scene shows the juxtaposition of Newham goods shed to Truro Cathedral and the city (left background). In this busy scene there are plenty of goods wagons visible and one is being unloaded on to a waiting lorry. For many years the site was served by a daily train but after a local gasworks siding closed the entire site was abandoned, in November 1971.** *Brunel University*

From the date of opening the line from Plymouth and Saltash to Truro was broad gauge. However it was not until 1866 (for freight) and 1867 (for passengers) that dual gauge track was in use between Truro and Penzance. From that time until abolished in 1892 broad gauge dominated the Cornish railway scene. In March 1891 there was a 'Great Blizzard' in west Cornwall and 'The Dutchman' from Paddington to Penzance, hauled by 4-4-0ST *Leopold*, was derailed near Stray Park, Camborne.
P. Q. Treloar Collection

absorbed the CR in 1876 and took over the Bristol & Exeter and South Devon Railways and as a consequence there were frequent changes in motive power. GWR 2-4-0T and tender engines also worked westwards into Cornwall.

Dean had designed two classes of tank engine that were capable of being converted from broad to narrow gauge when the time (inevitably) came. They were 2-4-0Ts and 0-4-2STs, although some of the former were converted to tender engines and all of the latter to 0-4-4STs, due to rough riding. Many other classes of GWR locomotive appeared and due to shortages in the west some standard gauge locomotives were converted to broad gauge to fill the gap! Some of Armstrong's standard 0-6-0 double-framed goods engines were similarly treated. Except for the convertibles, all of the old Bristol & Exeter and South Devon Railway locomotives, which were mostly 4-4-0STs, were scrapped in 1892 when the broad gauge was abandoned. From that date Cornish main line traffic was worked by standard GWR engines.

From 1895 most passenger trains were hauled by various classes of 4-4-0 that seemed ideally suited to the task in Cornwall, especially the 'Duke' class and later the 'Bulldog' class. Larger-wheeled 'Badminton', 'Atbara' and 'City' class 4-4-0s normally worked between Plymouth and Paddington.

Photographs of broad gauge locomotives and trains in Cornwall are not particularly common and are likely to be published on more than one occasion. This situation has been avoided where possible but not in the case of this fine view of broad gauge 0-6-0ST No 2165 *Achilles*. Built by the Avonside Engine Company for the South Devon Railway (SDR) in 1873, the locomotive was transferred to the Great Western Railway (GWR) and converted to standard gauge in 1893, becoming No 1324. The immaculate machine, footplate crew and depot staff are seen at the second Penzance running shed. *P. Q. Treloar Collection*

This is a very significant and truly historic photograph, which shows the very last broad gauge train at Truro in May 1892. The train is headed by a curious pair, GWR 0-6-0ST No 1256, a convertible of 1877, and No 3557, a GWR 0-4-4 back tank. Both locomotives were subsequently converted to standard gauge but within a couple of days the broad gauge would never be seen again. Note the unusual pedestrian bridge and the water tower.
Courtesy Maurice Dart

electrics began to appear; initially Class 45/46 1Co-Co1 'Peaks', mainly on inter-regional trains from about 1967, followed by 2,750hp (later re-rated to 2,580hp) Class 47s and, in 1971, 1,250hp Class 25s, which finally replaced the Class 22s. The arrival of further Class 47s resulted in the extinction of the B-B 'Warships', the originals having been withdrawn as early as 1969. At the very end of 1974 the first English Electric Class 50s arrived, having been transferred from the London Midland Region following the electrification of the West Coast main line. As more came on-line the non-electrical train heating Class 52s were gradually withdrawn, the last surviving until February 1977.

From 1978 the reliable 1,750hp English Electric Class 37s arrived in Cornwall and they in turn replaced the Class 25s. They were used primarily on freight workings and became synonymous with china clay trains. Their reign was to last more than 20 years until high-tech North American-built Class 66s made an appearance at the end of 1999. From May 1980 IC125 High Speed Train units replaced locomotive-hauled trains on London workings and later cross-country trains, having first been used on certain titled trains in 1979. Class 46s and later Class 45s disappeared from the railway scene in the 1980s and by the beginning of the 1990s locomotive-hauled passenger trains, except for the overnight sleepers and excursion workings, were rapidly becoming a thing of the past. By 1992 the last Class 50 was withdrawn and savage inroads were made into the ranks of Class 47s. Class 57s made regular appearances in Cornwall on the overnight sleepers, for a while marketed as the 'Night Riviera'. In the 1990s Class 60 locomotives appeared on some of the long-distance air-braked freights and in 2004 streamlined Class 220/221 'Voyager' units started working inter-regional trains, by then marketed as 'Cross Country' by the eponymous Virgin Trains TOC. Class 67 locomotives worked some postal trains in Cornwall until the abandonment of the latter. Special workings have brought Classes 20, 31, 33, 40, 55 and 56 into the Royal Duchy from time to time and steam-hauled specials have produced some classes of locomotive that were not historically indigenous to Cornwall. However, most of the second generation of diesel locomotives have now been withdrawn. Over the years, Class 03, 04, 08, 09 and 10 shunters worked minor lines and sidings.

It should be mentioned that the Cornish branch lines were worked by a quite remarkable mix of locomotives, many with obscure origins. Goods trains were worked by either 0-6-0 locomotives of Dean and Armstrong designs or saddle tanks on the shorter runs, although from about 1909 'Aberdare' 2-6-0s started to arrive in the Duchy. Both the '44xx' and '45xx' 2-6-2 prairie tanks were also being employed in Cornwall in large numbers. The 'Bulldogs' and 'Dukes' started to disappear from Cornwall as Churchward '43xx' class 2-6-0s came on stream and this purposeful class worked both passenger and freight traffic.

There had always been weight restrictions placed upon the size of locomotives that could work into Cornwall. However, after the Royal Albert Bridge had been strengthened in 1908 and the wooden trestle at Penzance had been replaced in 1921 (plus of course the viaduct rebuilding programme already mentioned) 'Saint' and 'Star' class 4-6-0s started to appear on the most prestigious trains. Large '31xx' class prairie tanks started work in Cornwall in 1912 and during and after the First World War heavy '28xx' and Railway Operating Department (ROD) '30xx' class 2-8-0s appeared. From 1929 'Hall' class 4-6-0s were the mainstay of Cornish train services, supplemented by the 'Grange' class from 1936 and the fine 4 cylinder 'Castle' class. The lighter 'Manor' class 4-6-0s were later arrivals, in 1938. After the Second World War 'County' class 4-6-0s became regulars and for a short period of time in 1951 standard 'Britannia' class 4-6-2s appeared. Some chunky '42xx' class 2-8-0 and '72xx' class 2-8-2 tank locomotives worked in Cornwall on heavy freights, normally but not exclusively, in the St Blazey area. It should be mentioned that from time to time other classes of steam locomotive visited the Royal Duchy such as the London Midland & Scottish Railway (LMS) Class 8F 2-8-0s. However, steam in Cornwall was gradually being replaced and by 1962 all steam locomotives had either been withdrawn or transferred away. Until comparatively recent times the heavy and powerful 'King' class 4-6-0s, with restricted route availability, were not officially allowed to cross the Royal Albert Bridge.

In main line terms diesel traction was first used in Cornwall in early 1958 when the original heavy A1A-A1A twin-engined 2,000hp North British 'Warship' class diesel hydraulics appeared. They were followed by the lighter Class 42/43 B-B 2,200hp 'Warships' and the small B-B 1,000/1,100hp Class 22s. Next to arrive in 1962 were the superb 2,700hp Class 52 'Western' C-C locomotives, which would haul the majority of express trains in the Duchy for nearly 15 years. Class 35 'Hymeks' made brief appearances during 1965/66. Diesel

Although multiple units have worked mainly on branches they have also been part of the main line scene since 1960. For some 30 years diesel mechanical units of various types and configurations dominated the scene but from the 1980s Classes 142, 150, 153, 155, 156 and 158 formed the multiple-unit mainstay of Cornish operations. It seems that in future the only interest in motive power will lie in new sub-classes, levels of refurbishment and the actual liveries of the various TOCs and ROSCOs.

Above: **This magnificent view of a broad gauge 4-4-0 tank locomotive also features a rather substantial driver, complete with mandatory watch chain! No 2132, formerly *Etna* of the SDR, was built by Rothwell in 1864 for the Carmarthen & Cardigan Railway. It was acquired by the SDR in 1868 and taken into GWR stock in 1876. It is remarkable to think of such locomotives working through Cornwall in the winter with no cab protection, which today really would give ASLEF something serious to complain about!**
Ian Allan Library/Bucknall Collection

Middle: **This superb shot shows broad gauge 4-4-0ST No 2125, which was built in 1866 by Slaughter Gruning to a Gooch design specially for the heavy gradients on the SDR. The construction was peculiar in that the boiler formed the connecting link between the cylinders and the main engine frame. Seen here as SDR *Sol*, the locomotive was absorbed by the GWR in 1876. Members of the class regularly worked on the Cornish main line.**
Ian Allan Library/Bucknall Collection

Right: **Although of dubious quality this photograph shows a very rare machine that was constructed in the Carn Brea works of the WCR, based on a Stothert & Slaughter design. Built in Cornwall as a standard gauge 0-6-0 in 1865, *Redruth* was acquired by the SDR and rebuilt as an 0-6-0ST and converted to broad gauge at Newton Abbot in 1871. It subsequently spent its life shunting at Millbay Docks, Plymouth, before being withdrawn in June 1887.** *Ian Allan Library/ Bucknall Collection*

Above: **The dual gauge track at Redruth is testimony to an 1866 or later dateline. However this view of broad gauge 4-4-0ST *Lance* is claimed to be the very first broad gauge train to work between Penzance and Truro in 1866 and the 'train' is an inspection coach for directors and dignitaries. The very tall chimney competes for attention with the two top-hatted gentlemen on the footplate.**
Cornish Studies Library

Below: **This magnificent view shows the Penzance terminus about 1878 in the days of a single passenger platform and dual gauge track. On the left is the goods shed, greatly enlarged since the 1852 opening, while on the right with the ships' masts above, is the original WCR engine shed, by this time superseded by the second structure just outside of the station. The visible goods wagons are all broad gauge, as is the SDR saddle tank locomotive on the right. Note the disc and crossbar signal at the platform end.**
Cornish Studies Library

Above: **In this fascinating shot at Gwinear Road station in 1888 a comparison can be made between the standard gauge Helston branch, left, and the dual gauge track main line, right. The branch line was opened in May 1887 and the broad gauge abolished in 1892. The main line through the station is little more than a passing loop with double track being provided from Camborne in 1900 and Angarrack in 1915. The signalbox on the right was replaced in 1915.** *Cornish Studies Library*

Below: **In retrospect it seems strange that the relatively small WCR company had a far more progressive future vision by adopting standard gauge, while the powerful Associated Companies, including the GWR, were still persevering with the incompatible and generally spurned broad gauge. The exact location of this crossing on the Cornish main line has not been determined but the splendid disc and crossbar signal should be noted.** *Royal Institution of Cornwall*

GREAT WESTERN RAILWAY

ALTERATION OF GAUGE

OF THE MAIN LINE

BETWEEN

EXETER AND TRURO

AND OF THE FOLLOWING

BRANCH LINES -

Newton Abbot and	Moretonhampstead	Tavistock and	Launceston
Newton Abbot „	Kingswear	Truro „	Falmouth
Churston „	Brixham	St. Erth „	St. Ives
Totnes „	Ashburton		

NOTICE IS HEREBY GIVEN that the lines of the Company between the above-mentioned points will be altered from the broad to the narrow gauge commencing on the night of Friday, May 20th, 1892.

During the time the alteration is being made the Lines specified will be closed, and all traffic upon them entirely suspended until the work is completed, which is expected to be on the night of Sunday, May 22nd.

In connection with the alteration of the Gauge, the following special arrangements will be in operation:—

PASSENGER TRAFFIC.

FRIDAY, MAY 20th.

The 10.15 a.m. Train from Paddington will call at several additional Stations as far as Plymouth and at all Stations beyond Plymouth.

The 11.45 a.m. Train from Paddington will not run beyond Plymouth.

The 5.0 p.m. Train from Plymouth to Penzance will not be run.

The running of some of the Branch Trains West of Plymouth will be altered.

SATURDAY, MAY 21st.

The ordinary Train Service between Penzance and Truro, and on the Helston Branch will be discontinued, and a special service of Passenger Trains will be in force.

SUNDAY, MAY 22nd.

No Trains will be run between Penzance and Truro, or between Plymouth and Tavistock.

MAIL TRAIN ARRANGEMENTS.

The 9.0 p.m. Mail Train from Paddington on Friday, May 20th, Saturday, 21st, and Sunday, 22nd, and the 8.23 p.m. Up Mail Train from Plymouth on Saturday, May 21st, and Sunday, 22nd, will be run between Exeter and Plymouth (North Road) via the London and South Western Company's route; the Up Mail will be due to leave North Road for Paddington at 8.30 p.m.

On Monday, May 23rd, the Night Mail Train will be run from Plymouth (North Road) to Penzance, leaving North Road at 4.40 a.m., and calling at all Stations. This Train will be in continuation of the Mail Train leaving Paddington at 9.0 p.m., on Sunday, May 22nd.

A STEAMER will be run between Plymouth and Falmouth on Saturday, May 21st and Sunday, 22nd, in connection with the London Night Mail Trains, calling at Fowey. 1st and 2nd Class Passengers will be booked locally by this Steamer.

GOODS TRAFFIC.

Intending Senders of Coal, Mineral, General Goods and other traffic to and from Stations between Exeter and Penzance, including Branches, are requested to take notice that the Company will not be able to receive traffic for conveyance to or from Stations on that section of the Railway, for a short period prior to Friday, May 20th, until after the conversion has taken place.

PLYMOUTH TRAFFIC.—By arrangement with the London and South Western Company an uninterrupted communication for General Goods Traffic will be maintained between Plymouth and Stations East of Exeter (inclusive), during the alterations.

For full particulars see Pamphlets, which can be obtained at the Stations.

Paddington, April, 1892.   HY. LAMBERT, General Manager

JUDD & Co., Limited, Printers, 63, Carter Lane, Doctors' Commons, E.C.   8859e

Above: **By the 1880s the abolition of the broad gauge had been on the cards for many years and during that decade the GWR had opted for standard gauge when constructing Cornish branch lines. Once the decision had been made to abolish the broad gauge a major logistical exercise was planned over the weekend of 21-23 May 1892. In this view workers are seen converting the gauge at the original St Germans Viaduct in east Cornwall.**
Ian Allan Library/Bucknall Collection

Left: **Between daybreak on Saturday, 21 May and 4am on Monday, 23 May 1892 a total of 177 route miles of track were converted by a massive workforce of 4,200 navvies. This rare survivor details all of the lines to be converted, including the main line and seven branches. The task was completed successfully; an object lesson in planning for Network Rail?** *Brunel University*

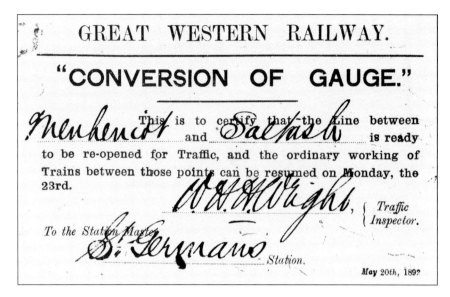

GREAT WESTERN RAILWAY.

"CONVERSION OF GAUGE."

Menheniot This is to certify that the Line between and *Saltash* is ready to be re-opened for Traffic, and the ordinary working of Trains between those points can be resumed on Monday, the 23rd.

W.H.Wright, { Traffic
{ Inspector.

To the Station Master
St Germans Station.

May 20th, 1892

Left: Another amazing Cornish survivor is this authorisation addressed to the Station Master at St Germans, confirming that the line between Menheniot and Saltash was ready to be reopened for traffic on Monday, 23 May 1892, following the completion of gauge conversion. The paper is signed by the responsible GWR Traffic Inspector, Mr Wright. *Ian Allan Library*

Below: In this exceptional 1892 view the complexities of a change of gauge at Truro are well illustrated. At a glance the scene appears to be chaotic but with so many lines and points to convert at this major railway location the area was bound to resemble a builders yard. The exercise is clearly labour-intensive with a complete absence of machinery and only a pickaxe and inching bar visible by way of tools of trade! *Royal Institution of Cornwall*

Right: One of the most remarkable WCR locomotives was the diminutive Avonside 0-4-0ST *Fox.* Purchased by the WCR for £750 in 1872 for shunting on the extensive Hayle wharves, the little 18-ton engine was absorbed by the GWR in 1876, whereupon it became No 1391. It was sold to the Gloucester Railway Carriage & Wagon Company in 1912 and it survived until 1948, when it was scrapped. *Author's Collection*

Above: **One of the most famous Cornish pioneers in the development of the steam engine was Richard Trevithick (1771-1833). He is attributed with the invention of the high pressure steam engine, a road locomotive and the world's first successful railway locomotive. In the circumstances it is hardly surprising that over the years a number of locomotives and units have been named after him. In this view an immaculate 'Duke' class 4-4-0 No 3270 *Trevithick* is seen at the second Penzance engine shed.**
P. Q. Treloar Collection

Below: **Over the years many GWR/WR locomotives have carried Cornish names, including the famous 4-4-0 *City of Truro*. Even in the diesel era names such as *City of Truro* and *Restormel Castle* have been carried by Class 47s and Class 37s have had a range of Cornish names, including *St Blazey Depot* and *Tre Pol and Pen*. A much earlier example of the latter name appeared on 'Duke' class 4-4-0 No 3265, which was rebuilt in January 1930 with straight 'Bulldog' frames, as seen here. The locomotive was withdrawn in December 1949.** *Ian Allan Library/Real Photographs*

2

Royal Albert Bridge

The Royal Albert Bridge pre-dates the adjacent road bridge across the River Tamar by more than 100 years. The magnificent structure is celebrating its 150th anniversary in 2009 and all of the indications are that it will continue to provide the main line rail link between Cornwall and the rest of the UK for the foreseeable future. The bridge is a distinctive structure and something of an icon, complemented by its long curved approaches on both sides of the river.

Building the bridge was not easy. There was some difficulty in finding bedrock that was capable of supporting the weight of the main central pier. In 1849 the engineer I. K. Brunel used a long metal tube that was lowered through the water and the mud to locate firm ground on the bed of the river. The water was then pumped out of the cylinder on diving bell principles to enable

Although photography had been invented by the mid-19th century the literate public had to rely on journals such as the *Illustrated London News* to gain a visual impression of reported news events. In this wonderful etching crowds are seen cheering the first up passenger train to cross the Royal Albert Bridge in May 1859. The actual caption on page 476 of the 14 May 1859 issue states 'Inauguration of the Albert Viaduct at Saltash by the Prince Consort'. *Author's Collection*

trial borings to be made. With costs escalating Brunel had to redesign the bridge to a single-track specification to save money. The construction work was let to contract in the sum of £162,000 but the contractor soon went bankrupt and Brunel decided that he would construct the bridge himself, at least in project management terms. Brunel's influence was considerable and with the backing of the railway company His Royal Highness Prince Albert agreed to the bridge being named after him.

A huge 300-ton cylinder that was 35ft in diameter and 95ft long was assembled on the banks of the river on the Devon side and when completed it was floated out to the centre of the river and sunk vertically on to its site in June 1854. It took some time for the tube to become seated on solid rock and for it then to be positioned 'dead plumb'. Its bottom edge was 87½ft below the high-water mark. Four cast-iron columns for the central pier were raised, which were octagonal in shape, 10ft in diameter and 100ft high, each weighing some 100 tons.

The main trusses were also constructed on the edge of the river beside two temporary quays also on the Devon side. Each truss was a 12ft 3in by 16ft 9in elliptical tube, strengthened internally by forged wrought-iron webs and externally by a series of metal plates and angle irons. The centres of the main arches were 56ft deep and the two ends 455ft apart. This weight

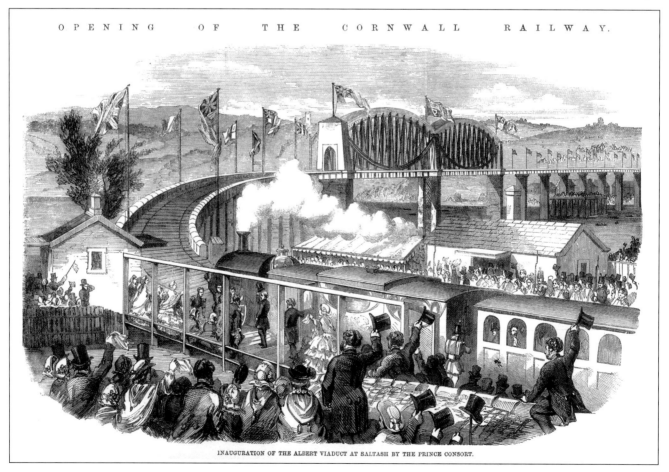

OPENING OF THE CORNWALL RAILWAY.

INAUGURATION OF THE ALBERT VIADUCT AT SALTASH BY THE PRINCE CONSORT.

This old 1859 print shows a broad gauge train leaving Cornwall and about to cross the Royal Albert Bridge, thereby entering the County of Devon. Workmen seem to be putting some finishing touches to the bridge, while the foreground seems to be quite rural, compared with the busy car park now located on this site.
The print is effectively celebrating a remarkable engineering achievement that is still in daily use, 150 years later.
Brunel University

was supported by huge chains. Each truss was a combination of an arch and a suspension bridge, the outward thrust of the arch on the abutments being counter balanced by the inward drag of the chains. The wrought iron work in each span weighed 1,600 tons. On 1 September 1857 the first of the two great trusses was ready for floating out onto the river using four iron pontoons. The pontoons carried a substantial timber frame comprising 40ft-long shores designed to carry 500/600 tons, half the weight of each truss. Warps, radial lines and capstans were used to prevent the truss from drifting down river.

Up to 40,000 people and 500 workers were on hand to witness the floating, as the day was declared a holiday in the local area. The process for partially sinking the pontoons, lifting the truss 100 feet above the water and jacking it into place was complex but carefully planned. The truss was jacked up at a rate of six feet per week and it was in position by July 1858. Brunel conducted the first exercise but the floating and positioning of the second truss was attended to by the resident engineer Mr R. P. Brereton, due to Brunel's ill health and absence abroad. The process went without a hitch and the second truss reached its final position in March 1859.

The finishing of the bridge amounted to far more than 'finishing touches' and much heavy engineering and construction work had to be completed, including building up the land piers and approach spans that comprised metal girders resting on granite piers, ten on the Cornish side and seven on the Devon side. The final vital statistics were impressive with two 455ft trusses, a total length of 2,200ft and containing 2,650 tons of wrought iron, 1,200 tons of cast iron, 459,000 cubic feet of masonry and 14,000 cubic feet of timber being used in its construction. The completion of the bridge was a major objective achieved but sadly Brunel was too ill to attend the

opening ceremony, and although he subsequently glimpsed his magnificent bridge he died on 5 September 1859.

A test train ran over the bridge on 11 April 1859 and the formal opening by HRH Prince Albert was on 2 May 1859. Special platforms were constructed on both sides of the river, on the Devon side for the Royal party and on the Cornwall side for distinguished guests. Rather grand speeches were made, followed by notable attendees joining the special Royal train that slowly crossed the bridge towards Cornwall, the local battery firing a Royal Salute as the train passed the central pier. The train passed through Saltash station and onto Coombe by Saltash Viaduct in order to view the Royal Albert Bridge from a fine vantage point. The train returned to Saltash whereupon Prince Albert walked across the bridge inspecting the works. He then examined the bridge from beneath, before boarding the two-funnel admiralty paddle steamer *Vivid*. After inspecting some fortifications at Tregantle, Prince Albert returned to Millbay Docks and after a 'substantial luncheon' he departed from Plymouth Millbay station for London at 7pm, arriving at Windsor at 1am!

Although in its day the bridge was an engineering miracle, and notwithstanding the 15mph speed limit across the bridge, the weight of locomotives and trains increased over the years requiring the bridge to be substantially strengthened in 1908 and 1927. In the 1930s there was extensive girder replacement on the approach spans and in 1969 significant work was needed to renovate the bridge to ensure it remained fit for purpose in the late 20th century. This work included strengthening the two main trusses and the vertical ties as well as providing additional horizontal bracing. From 1961 the structure was overshadowed in size but not style by the opening of the Tamar road bridge. Upon the opening of the road bridge the 1833 Saltash Ferry ceased operations. During the centenary celebrations in 1959 the Royal Albert Bridge was floodlit for a season to celebrate the event and in 2007 an ugly walkway, seemingly comprised of scaffolding, was removed to clearly reveal the legend 'I.K. Brunel – Engineer – 1859'.

Following the closure of the Bude branch line, the North Cornwall Railway line and the GW Launceston branch in the 1960s the only other railway crossing between Devon and Cornwall is across the single-track Calstock Viaduct that spans the River Tamar above the town of the same name. This branch line remains open but only as far as Gunnislake. Thus the Royal Albert Bridge survives as the only significant rail link into and out of Cornwall and is a very fitting starting point for our journey along Cornwall's main line.

Left: **It is fascinating to consider how, without the benefit of modern technology, two vast bridge trusses could be positioned on their piers some 100 feet above the water level. The 1,000 ton-plus trusses were floated out onto the River Tamar using four giant pontoons. The trusses were jacked-up into place at a rate of 6 feet per week! The positioning of the second truss, seen here in 1858, was overseen by I. K. Brunel's resident engineer R. P. Brereton, due to the great man's ill health.**
Royal Institution of Cornwall

Below: **At first glance the photographer has taken his life in his hands by adopting a highly vulnerable position to photograph No 5023 *Brecon Castle* entering Cornwall with the down 'Cornishman' on 26 May 1956. However he was there under supervision during a Plymouth Railway Circle visit, in the days before the current obsession with health and safety matters. Nowadays the single line across the bridge is controlled by Plymouth signalling panel.** *R. T. Coxon*

Above: **In the Victorian era the dimensions of the Royal Albert Bridge were almost beyond belief and they still make impressive reading. The two main trusses are 455ft long, the total bridge length is 2,200ft, it contains 2,650 tons of wrought iron (since replaced by mild steel spans), 1,200 tons of cast iron and 459,000 cubic feet of masonry. In this view the diesel era in Cornwall is about to commence as original 2,000hp 'Warship' No D600 *Active* heads the 'Cornish Riviera' across the bridge on 25 April 1958.** *British Railways*

Below: **During 1959 the Royal Albert Bridge celebrated its centenary and for some weeks the magnificent structure was floodlit, resulting in the publication of locally produced postcards. Just two years later the purity of the view across the Tamar was compromised when a new road bridge opened, resulting in the discontinuance of the famous Saltash ferry, which had been in continuous operation since 1833.** *Author's Collection*

35/23　Saltash, Royal Albert Bridge, built by I. K. Brunel in 1859.

Right: **Another notable event to celebrate the centenary of the Royal Albert Bridge was the commissioning of a poster by the Public Relations Office of the Western Region of British Railways. The poster was based on a painting by the famous artist Terence Cuneo. 'Castle' class No 5021** *Whittington Castle* **is entering Cornwall with a down express.** *British Railways*

Below: **This utterly fascinating working dates back to 29 April 1962 and shows two green single power cars crossing from Cornwall to Devon with a local train for Plymouth but with two six-wheeled milk tankers coupled to the train. It is thought that these were added to the train at Saltash and so their journey would be a short one! Note the Southern Region lines on the right, which at this time was their main line to Okehampton, Exeter and Waterloo.** *Brian Haresnape*

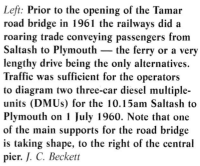

Left: **Prior to the opening of the Tamar road bridge in 1961 the railways did a roaring trade conveying passengers from Saltash to Plymouth — the ferry or a very lengthy drive being the only alternatives. Traffic was sufficient for the operators to diagram two three-car diesel multiple-units (DMUs) for the 10.15am Saltash to Plymouth on 1 July 1960. Note that one of the main supports for the road bridge is taking shape, to the right of the central pier.** *J. C. Beckett*

Middle: **Over the years the 'Grange' class 4-6-0s were real workhorses in Cornwall, working every type of train. With steam to spare No 6825 *Llanvair Grange* heads a very mixed freight off of the Royal Albert Bridge on 28 April 1962 at the regulation 15mph. One of the last tasks in completing the bridge was building up the land-based granite piers, ten on the Cornish side and seven on the Devon side of the main spans.** *Brian Haresnape*

Below: **In the days of steam many of the local trains that worked from Plymouth to Saltash, sometimes running as far as Liskeard, were operated in push-pull mode with auto trailers at either end of the centrally positioned 0-6-0 pannier tank. About to cross the Royal Albert Bridge on 13 April 1952 is a westbound four-coach train. The signalbox survives for use by bridge maintenance staff.** *R. E. Vincent*

Over the years the Royal Albert Bridge has received many modifications. In 1908 cross girders were incorporated to accommodate the increasing weight of trains. The wrought iron spans were replaced in 1928 and in 1968 additional horizontal bracing was provided and the main trusses and vertical ties were strengthened. In connection with the 1968 strengthening this rare photograph shows a bridge engineer adding weights to vulnerable points on this perspex model of the bridge, to simulate heavy trains crossing. Stress points in the vertical members were tested electronically. *British Railways Derby*

During 2006 an ugly metal walkway and associated scaffolding were removed from each end of the bridge to expose clearly the legend 'I.K. Brunel Engineer 1859'. Crossing the bridge in October 2006 is a Virgin Voyager forming an inter-regional 'Cross Country' train. Virgin Trains subsequently lost the 'XC' franchise, resulting in quite recent scenes such as this joining the annals of railway history. *Author*

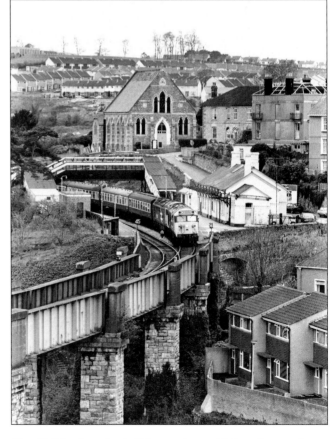

The old Saltash station building on the up side is unfortunately no longer in railway use and since this April 1983 photograph was taken the station overbridge has been demolished. The Baptist chapel burnt to the ground and developers eventually finished the new housing estate in the top background. Providing super power for the 11.05 Penzance to Plymouth are Nos 50034 *Furious* and No 50021 *Rodney*, which would soon be crossing the mighty River Tamar. *Author*

3

Saltash to Liskeard

S altash station is located at the Cornish end of the Royal Albert Bridge. The main buildings were on the up side of the line reflecting the direction that most passengers would be travelling. The surviving buildings, albeit no longer in railway use, date back to the 1880s and plans are in existence to utilise them as a museum, telling visitors the story of the opening of the railway. Originally the track layout at the station formed a passing loop and a signalbox was located halfway along the up platform, until it was closed in July 1973. Over the years two pedestrian overbridges were provided for passengers but the last was demolished in the 1980s. The up platform was extended in 1906. From 1876 a four-horse stagecoach ran between Saltash station and Callington and from 1904 an early GWR motorbus service worked the same route calling also at Albaston. To the west of the station was a two-road goods yard, latterly operated from a ground frame. For many years milk traffic was loaded in the sidings and, in addition to general goods, flowers were dispatched at the turn of the 20th century. The yard closed in 1963, although the sidings remained for a few years afterwards. In 1903 there were 14 staff at Saltash and this had grown to 21 by 1923, all in stark contrast to its 'unmanned' status from October 1971. For several decades Saltash was served by motor train locals from Plymouth and then by DMUs, until the Tamar road bridge opened in 1961. From the 1980s running in signs welcomed passengers to Saltash and Cornwall (see photographs).

Beyond Saltash station is Coombe by Saltash Viaduct, sometimes referred to as simply Coombe Viaduct. The original 603ft long 86ft high timber structure was replaced by a masonry example in 1894. In February 1906 the line from Saltash to Wearde signalbox was doubled and a goods loop was opened during the Second World War. Just beyond the signalbox was Defiance Platform, a halt that was opened in March 1905, re-sited in 1907 (as was the original signalbox) and closed on 27

October 1930. Just beyond Wearde the original 1859 line travelled alongside the shore of the River Lynher and crossed wooden viaducts, mostly on trestles across tidal inlets, as follows: Forder, 606ft long and 67ft high, Wivelscombe, 198ft long and 25ft high, Grove, 114ft long and 29ft high (the shortest viaduct on the main line), Nottar, 921ft long and 67ft high and St

Above: **During 1985/6 the Cornish Railways initiative was instigated whereby a degree of regional autonomy was afforded to a locally managed railway. Part of the enterprise included the erection of 'first' and 'last' station signs at Saltash, as photographed on 17 August 1986. The experiment was overtaken by events when BR sectorisation was introduced and certain activities were divided into accountable business sectors.** *Author*

Left: **Over the years the railway companies and the Cornwall County Council have collaborated in welcoming visitors and holidaymakers to the county. This bilingual sign was in situ at the up end of the up platform in October 2006, sponsored by the First Great Western company and Cornwall County Council. The public house in the background is appropriately named The Two Bridges.** *Author*

This Edwardian scene at Saltash shows two steam-powered railmotors comprising a local train from Plymouth, calling at the station to set down passengers. In the view are both up and down station buildings, substantial awnings, the second pedestrian footbridge and an up platform signalbox. Note the white two-storey building on the right. *Author's Collection*

Germans, 945ft long and 106ft high. A loop was created at Wivelscombe signalbox in 1898 and extended in 1904. There was also a signalbox to the east of St Germans Viaduct. After 50 years of service these original viaducts were showing signs of age and a new route to the north of the old alignment was surveyed.

An extremely rare visitor to Cornwall crossed the Royal Albert Bridge in August 1997, when a former Eastern Region greyhound in the shape of 'Deltic' Class 55 No D9000 *Royal Scots Grey* headed west with a Pathfinder Railtours 'chartex'. The green-liveried 3,300hp twin-engined machine was just opening the taps after its slowing to 15mph. The footbridges, station buildings and awnings have long gone but the white building seen above (and the Royal Albert Bridge!) have survived. *Author*

The new line opened for goods in March 1908 and for all traffic in May 1908, when the original line was abandoned, except for a short length used as a carriage siding at the Wearde end. Wearde signalbox closed in October 1965.

The new line ran across a new Forder Viaduct that is 699ft in length, which runs just below the local landmark of Trematon Castle. There was once a tidemill just to the south of the viaduct at Anthony Passage. The views from this viaduct and others further west are spectacular. Beyond Forder is the 451-yard Shillingham Tunnel (sometimes referred to as Wivelscombe Tunnel). There was a severe landslip at this location in 1942 that resulted in single-line running for nearly six months. The next viaduct is the 618ft long Nottar Viaduct (sometimes referred to

A scene that sadly shows a charming English era that has gone forever. With a family in summer dress visiting the Wymans newspaper kiosk on Saltash station and the novelty of a member of railway staff on the platform, the fireman of 0-6-0PT No 6400 replenishes its pannier tanks by the down side water column on 28 August 1961. This local auto train from Plymouth would soon be replaced by diesel mechanical units.
R. C. Riley/Transport Treasury

as Lynher Viaduct) that carries the line on a curve over the River Lynher. The line curves further west to cross the River Tiddy on the 'new' 1908 St Germans Viaduct, an impressive 978ft-long structure. A quay, a few cottages and an old limekiln are located in a picturesque setting below the viaduct. St Germans station is just west of the viaduct. Again the surviving main buildings are on the up side, although no longer railway-owned. The down side buildings are also intact. There was a goods yard that boasted a two-ton capacity crane at the up end of the up platform, which closed in 1965 and a holiday coach is presently located in an old goods bay loading platform. In 1930 a total of ten staff were employed at the station by the GWR. The down side signalbox was closed in 1973 but after that date, until closed in 1998, a signalling room was located on the down platform that had interface with Plymouth panel and Liskeard signalbox.

The line from St Germans through Trerulefoot to Tresulgan Viaduct climbs steeply with gradients of up to 1 in 68. This section was doubled in 1895. There was a signalbox at Trerule in Edwardian times and also between 1938 and 1954. East and West Tresulgan signalboxes closed about 1899. The original Margary Class A viaduct was 525ft long and 93ft high but it was replaced in 1899 by a new masonry viaduct. It should be mentioned that just before the Second World War some earthworks were prepared in this area for a proposed branch line that would have offered a direct route from St Germans to Looe but the idea was abandoned. The line continues westward through some pleasant undulating farmland peppered with valleys that the railway crosses majestically.

The next point of interest is Coldrennick Viaduct, which was rebuilt and the track doubled in 1898. During rebuilding in February 1897 there was a terrible accident when a working platform with 17 workers on it, which was suspended below the viaduct, broke away sending 12 men to their deaths as they hit the ground some 140 feet below. The platform had not been chained to the viaduct in accordance with safety regulations. Twenty-five children were orphaned as a result of the accident. The 795ft long and 138ft high viaduct had 12 fully buttressed masonry piers and was the fifth highest in Cornwall. As seen from the A38 the viaduct is still impressive. Just beyond Coldrennick is Menheniot station that has, perhaps surprisingly, remained open. The station is over a mile from the village it purports to serve, although there is a hamlet in the immediate

In this vintage scene at Saltash locals are posing for the camera on the up platform, which was extended in 1906, as a tank engine shunts the small goods yard beyond the bridge in the background. When this photograph was taken Saltash had a staff complement of 15. On the down side the goods yard closed in 1963, all staff were withdrawn in October 1971 and the door on the signalbox closed for the last time in July 1973.
Author's Collection

Above: **Beyond Saltash and Coombe by Saltash Viaduct was Defiance Platform, a small halt that opened in March 1905, was re-sited in 1907 and which closed in October 1930. The halt was at a location known as Wearde Quay and here Class 42 'Warship' No D829 *Magpie* passes Wearde signalbox with the down 'Royal Duchy' on 14 June 1961. No fewer than 14 naval warships and auxiliary vessels, including two aircraft carriers, are anchored off Devonport, which can be seen in the background.** *J. C. Beckett*

vicinity of the station. For many years the GWR advertised an omnibus connection from the station to the coastal town of Looe. A total of six staff were employed there in 1922 but the station became unstaffed in 1965. There is a signalbox on the down platform that was taken out of use in 1973 when sidings serving Clicker Tor Quarry on the down side were closed. The small goods yard at the west end of the down platform ceased operations in September 1963. Sadly the disused main station building on the down side burnt to the ground a few years ago. A delightful little waiting shelter remains on the up platform and there is an overbridge connecting the platforms, which are served by infrequent trains.

About a mile west of Menheniot station is Treviddo Viaduct, 486ft long and 101ft high. The single-track Margary Class A viaduct had a wooden fan top based on masonry piers but was replaced by an all-masonry viaduct in 1898. There was also an accident at Treviddo in 1897 when in November two men died during rebuilding as a result of some heavy wood swinging from the viaduct, which hit the two workmen. An east and west signalbox closed when the line was doubled in 1898. Just over a mile beyond Treviddo the line passes under the main A38 road and just beyond is Cartuther Viaduct, 411ft long and 89ft high. It too was completely replaced by a masonry viaduct but as early as 1882. At this point the main line continues to twist and turn

Above: **Rapidly approaching the site of Defiance Platform on 20 April 1985 is No 50016 *Barham* with the 09.40 Paddington to Penzance. These 2,700hp locomotives started to appear in Cornwall at the end of 1974 following their displacement from the London Midland Region, as a result of the electrification of the West Coast main line north of Crewe. Eventually nearby Plymouth Laira would have a sizeable allocation of Class 50s, a situation that continued until about 1992.** *Author*

One of the finest classes of steam locomotive that could be found working on GWR/WR lines in the County of Cornwall was the 'Castle' class 4-6-0. With the heavier 'King' class officially banned from crossing the Royal Albert Bridge the 'Castles' and some might say the 'County' class were the optimum power in passenger train terms, although the slightly less glamorous 'Grange' and 'Hall' class 4-6-0s put in some sprightly performances. Reliving the past on 6 September 1985 was No 7029 *Clun Castle* seen here near Defiance Platform with 'chartex' 1Z47, bound for Truro. The Royal Albert Bridge can just be glimpsed on the right.
Gavin Morrison

as indeed it does for much of the way between Saltash and Penzance, with only a few straight sections of track, causing Cornwall never to have any water troughs for the replenishment of steam locomotive tenders, unlike so many other main lines in the age of steam.

Heading towards Liskeard the next structure of note is Bolitho Viaduct, with the farm of the same name below, named after one of Cornwall's most famous families. The original was wooden topped with six masonry piers and was 546ft long and 113ft high. It was rebuilt in 1882 on the same alignment as the original by using two longitudinal sections so that traffic was not interrupted. The viaduct often features in railway photographs because just east of the viaduct a lower quadrant semaphore signal, Liskeard's outer, has since the 1980s been the first such signal encountered by a train travelling from either London or Birmingham to west Cornwall. With the line continuing its tortuous course the magnificent Liskeard Viaduct is reached, just to the east of Liskeard station. This fine structure stands 150ft above the ground and is 720ft long. It was rebuilt in 1894 with the existing nine masonry piers being extended in brick in order to support metal girders. These

When Brunel was called upon by the CR to plan a main line from Plymouth to Truro and Falmouth it soon became apparent that there were many obstacles to overcome, including numerous valleys and tidal inlets. To keep costs to a minimum he designed viaducts that made considerable use of wood, either by being of all wood construction or timber topped on masonry piers. In the former category was Coombe by Saltash Viaduct, seen here being replaced with a new masonry structure during 1894.
Cornish Studies Library

girders became corroded and they were replaced during another rebuilding in 1929, when new steel girders were put in place. Heavy maintenance work took place in 1924, before the rebuild, and also in 1949. A point of interest is that the original piers, which are still in use today, were of the same design as Moorswater and St Pinnock Viaducts except there were no Gothic openings. The line from Treviddo Viaduct to Liskeard was doubled in 1896. Far below the viaduct the single-track Looe branch line tumbles down towards Coombe Junction.

Liskeard station is of some importance not only because it serves a busy and growing market town but because since 1901 it has been the junction station for the coastal town of Looe. The branch line station is set at right angles to the main line station on the up (or north) side. There is a connecting rail link with the main line. In times gone by the link was with the down road but from 1981 the configuration has comprised a single-track connection from the up main line. The single track feed leads into a loop before reaching the single line down to Coombe Junction. A trailing connection serves the single branch platform. The main line station is located in a deep cutting and the main station building is located at street level high above the platforms. A main road straddles the cutting, from which there are fine views in both directions. There are up and down main line platforms with a connecting pedestrian overbridge. Until 1915 there was a signalbox part way along the up platform but this was replaced by a signalbox at the up end of the down platform. Until 1918 there was a small engine shed between the viaduct and the station on the down side. After the shed's closure two refuge sidings remained but they were lifted in the 1980s. On the up side there was a large goods shed and yard at the west end of the station as well as a loading dock, while at the east end was another goods handling area, adjacent to the spur leading onto the Looe branch. There were several additional sidings parallel to the branch platform, latterly used as engineers sidings. All goods traffic ceased at Liskeard in June 1981. The down platform was extended in 1937 and the up platform in 1984 and in 2006. Part of the main station building was completely replaced by a new 'glass and alloy' structure, also in 2006. There have been various generations of much smaller buildings and shelters on the down platform. The maximum staffing levels seems to have been in 1923 when 30 employees worked at Liskeard, covering shifts 24 hours per day. Liskeard retains its semaphore signals and much of its yesteryear atmosphere.

The telephoto lens accentuates the curve on the 86ft high Coombe by Saltash Viaduct. Catching the late afternoon light on 31 March 1986 is No 50037 *Illustrious* heading the 13.40 Paddington to Penzance. The locomotive is in 'large logo' livery and is fitted with snowploughs. In the background are the sheds of the erstwhile Saltash goods yard and some local allotments. *Author*

Above: **Although freight traffic in Cornwall is now at a rather low ebb, with a little patience the modern scene still has much to offer. On 5 October 2007 green and yellow-liveried Railfreight Heavy Haul Class 66 No 66622 rolls off of Coombe by Saltash Viaduct and into Saltash station with 6Z66, a Burngullow to Angerstein Wharf sand train, the sand being a waste product of the china clay filtering and drying process.** *Author*

Middle: **A flashback to April 1993 finds a now discontinued freight flow leaving Coombe by Saltash Viaduct and passing the old goods yard site. The train is the much-lamented (by railway enthusiasts) weekly fertiliser empties from Truro to Ince & Elton. On this day the train was hauled by original Railfreight-liveried No 47337 with five cargowaggons and a Kemira Fertilisers wagon in tow. The United Kingdom Fertilisers contract was lost to road, with the former customer not only saving money but controlling all aspects of distribution while retaining maximum flexibility.** *Author*

Left: **A final pleasantly framed view of Coombe by Saltash Viaduct and the two Tamar bridges finds two single power car Gloucester DMUs in green livery, with front end 'whiskers', heading west with a local working on 29 April 1962. These units could be found at work in the Royal Duchy for the next 30 years!** *Brian Haresnape*

Above: **Cornwall at its best on 20 October 1988, as a Class 155 'Sprinter' DMU crosses the 699ft-long Forder Viaduct at high tide with the 12.50 Penzance to Cardiff. In the background is the local landmark of Trematon Castle. On the right is Antony Passage mill stream dam, which was built in 1465 to power the tidemill on the left.** *Author*

Middle: **This scene depicts the 618-ft long Nottar Viaduct, sometimes referred to as Lynher Viaduct, which spans the River Lynher. Looking diminutive compared with the fine masonry structure, is single power car No M55012 forming the 15.24 Liskeard to Plymouth working on 20 October 1988. This viaduct is located on a new main line alignment that came into use during 1908, when the original route to the south was abandoned.** *Author*

Right: **One of the more impressive viaducts on the Cornish main line is the 978ft-long St Germans Viaduct, best seen from the approach road to the old quay. The viaduct carries the main line over the River Tiddy, which can just be glimpsed in the foreground. A Regional Railways 700hp Class 158 unit makes for Penzance in August 1997.** *Author*

Left: **Looking somewhat dilapidated in this April 1990 photograph, the main station buildings at St Germans have nevertheless survived the passage of time. Although now unmanned, back in 1930 no fewer than ten staff looked after the needs of passengers, their luggage and other goods. There was a signalbox on the down side but this closed in 1973, from which time a 'signalling room' in a building on the down platform had interface with Plymouth panel and Liskeard signalbox. Passing the station at speed is the 12.10 Penzance to Crewe vans headed by InterCity-liveried No 47625.** *Author*

Middle: **During 1989 an important new freight flow was introduced whereby china clay slurry was transported in new 90-tonne bogie tank wagons from Burngullow to Irvine in Scotland for use in the paper-making industry. By 1999 one million tonnes had been conveyed by what had become known as the 'Silver Bullet' train. With a standard 11-wagon freight in tow a brace of Class 37s, in original and new Railfreight livery, cross Tresulgan Viaduct with the up working, in April 1990.** *Author*

Below: **This fine view shows 'Hall' class 4-6-0 No 7925 *Westol Hall* with the 1.30pm Paddington to Penzance passing the goods yard at St Germans station on 16 July 1956. Served by a two-ton crane, the goods yard was located between the viaduct and the station and it survived until 1965. The down goods loop on the right was lifted many years ago.** *R. C. Riley/Transport Treasury*

Right: An illustrated history of the Cornish main line would not be complete without at least one photograph of the viaducts on the original pre-1908 alignment between Wearde Quay and St Germans. This 1899 view shows the 606ft-long, 67ft-high Forder Viaduct, south of the current masonry structure. The viaduct was a wooden Margary Class C type and to the west of this location were Wivelscombe, Grove, Nottar and St Germans Viaducts. After nearly 50 years of service they all needed replacement, subsequently being demolished after the opening of the new line. *Cornish Studies Library*

Middle: Leaving the 93ft-high Tresulgan Viaduct with a very mixed up freight in the 1950s is No 6305, one of Churchward's mixed traffic moguls that were first introduced in 1911. For more than 40 years these purposeful 2-6-0s could be seen on a variety of trains throughout Cornwall. No 6305 was a St Blazey engine and there is a good chance that the freight originated from that location. *Cornish Studies Library*

Below: The 1,750hp English Electric Class 37s began to appear in Cornwall in 1979 and they were to be the mainstay of Cornish freight workings for more than 20 years. About the time of their arrival most main-line freight wagons were fitted with air brakes, whereas the local china clay wagons, which survived until 1988, were vacuum braked. Dual-braked Nos 37420 *The Scottish Hosteller* in Mainline livery and No 37670 in 'triple grey' Railfreight livery are seen approaching Bethany, near Doddycross, on 8 April 1991 with the 15.45 St Blazey to Gloucester Speedlink service. *Author*

Left: **In railway enthusiast circles Cornwall was always well known for its van trains, which included newspaper, postal, parcel and perishable workings. All have now ceased but on 22 September 1994 the up 14.00 Penzance to Redhill vans was a survivor. Rail express systems-liveried No 47776 *Respected* is seen just east of Tresulgan Viaduct.** *Author*

Middle: **At 795ft in length and standing 138ft above the ground Coldrennick Viaduct is an impressive structure. It was rebuilt in 1898, when the track was doubled. During rebuilding in February 1897 there was a terrible accident when a working platform that had not been properly chained to the viaduct broke away, sending 12 men to their deaths in the valley below. The event was a talking point locally for many years and the writer of this postcard, postally used from Liskeard to Shrewsbury in 1902, mentions the fact.** *Author's Collection*

MENHENIOT VIADUCT

From this Viaduct, in the centre during repairs, twelve men fell & were killed. M.S.&L.C. Nov 4th 1902

Below: **When photographed 90 years after the disaster Coldrennick Viaduct looked very much the same, although the girders seem to have been replaced. The brick extensions to the masonry piers that replaced the old wooden superstructure can clearly be seen as Network SouthEast Class 50 No 50019 *Ramillies* heads west with the 07.00 Milton Keynes to Penzance on 13 June 1987.** *Author*

Right: **Beyond Coldrennick Viaduct is Menheniot station, which is over a mile from the village of the same name. Of interest in this 1950s view are the up starting signal on the down side, the original station building, Clicker Tor Quarry (top left), the passenger footbridge connecting the platforms and the signalbox, which closed in 1973. One of the versatile 'Hall' class 4-6-0s, No 7916 *Mobberley Hall*, passes with the 1.20pm from Penzance to Paddington on 16 July 1956.** *Cornish Studies Library*

Left: **Menheniot station became unstaffed as long ago as 1965 and without supervision it was almost inevitable that the station would become vandalised, and finally burnt to the ground. Behind the old signalbox on the left was a small goods yard, as well as the sidings serving the Clicker Tor Quarry. The yard closed in 1963. Running through the reverse curves west of the station and passing the attractive up side shelter on 25 July 1986 is No 50024 *Vanguard* with the 10.00 Penzance to Paddington.** *Author*

Right: **This large '51xx' class 2-6-2T Prairie, No 5148, is seen working hard with a down freight near Trerulefoot in east Cornwall. These tank engines were 1928 Collett rebuilds of an earlier Churchward design. They weighed more than a 'Hall' class locomotive (ex-tender) and compared with the smaller '45xx' class prairie tanks they were 20 tons heavier and had driving wheels that were over one foot larger in diameter.** *Cornish Studies Library*

Above: **One of the staple commodities conveyed by rail from the early days of the railway until 1980 was milk. Sidings at St Erth, Dalcoath, Lostwithiel, Saltash and others all contributed, with the milk being conveyed in 3,000 gallon six-wheeled tank wagons. Here No 5985 *Mostyn Hall* leaves Liskeard with the 12.35pm Sunday Penzance to Kensington milk train. Most trains were unloaded at either Kensington or West Ealing.** *Author's Collection*

Below: **No 5148 seems to have been a very active locomotive in Cornwall during the 1950s, which is hardly surprising considering its allocation to Plymouth Laira. Coming off Liskeard Viaduct the locomotive is heading a mixed westbound freight. The photographer has framed the train between two wonderful wooden-post lower quadrant semaphore signals, controlled by the nearby Liskeard signalbox.** *R. C. Riley/Transport Treasury*

Above: **One of the most pleasant photographic locations in Cornwall is a minor road overbridge to the east of Liskeard, just beyond Bolitho Viaduct, where the view of up trains is uninterrupted. This very newsworthy event occurred on 2 September 1988 when No 43182, the leading power car of this IC125 unit, suffered a broken windscreen. This resulted in the 16.25 Penzance to Paddington being piloted by Network SouthEast-liveried No 50001 *Dreadnought*. The rear power car is on Bolitho Viaduct.** *Author*

Below: **Hardly comparable with the days of the broad gauge is this photograph of North American super power at Bolitho Viaduct on 15 June 2006. Direct Rail Services No 66407 was on hire to Freightliner Heavy Haul to work 6M37, the 15.30 Moorswater to Earles sidings. The Cumbrian-based interloper is seen powering a total of 21 empty cement tankers eastward.** *Sam Felce*

Above: **Introduced in 1999/2000, the Spanish-built General Motors Class 67s were set to invade Cornwall for what, in retrospect, was a very brief period of time. These 125mph 2,980hp machines were imported to operate postal services as part of a new fast network, linked to a major distribution centre at Willesden. Catching the late afternoon sunshine at Bolitho in September 2002 was No 67010, working the all-red liveried train from St Blazey to Plymouth.** *Author*

Left: **Since the end of the 1980s the lower quadrant semaphore signal on the left, which is Liskeard's outer home signal, has been the first semaphore signal to be encountered on a journey from London to Cornwall! Crossing Bolitho Viaduct as the driver activates the windscreen washers is a Virgin Voyager forming the 09.30 Penzance to Glasgow on a sunny 5 October 2007.** *Author*

Above: With the early morning sun glinting off the side of a Par-bound DMU and with mist lingering in the valley beyond, a local service from Plymouth arrives at Liskeard station in October 1991. On the up road the short semaphore starting signal and the advanced starter are both off but the signalman has already restored his down home signal. Note the guide rails on Liskeard Viaduct, centre left. *Author*

Below: Another early morning shot finds large logo-liveried No 47616 *Y Ddraig Goch/The Red Dragon* heading the overnight 21.46 Leeds to Penzance vans crossing the 720ft long and 150ft high Liskeard Viaduct. On the left the Looe branch line can be seen, which descends initially to Coombe Junction. *Author*

Left: This pair of photographs shows 'up' trains at both the up and down platforms at Liskeard station. By Sunday 4 September 1988 No 50012 *Benbow* had been relegated from express passenger to engineering train duties and the locomotive was in fact withdrawn shortly after this scene was recorded. The train comprises assorted ballast wagons and a 'shark' brake van. *Author*

Middle: The Liskeard signalman on the left has given the road to 'triple-grey'-liveried No 37673, which eases its train of empty CDA wagons from the main line onto the Looe branch for the trip down to ECC Moorswater china clay works for loading. The speed limit at this point is 5mph. For a time some of the Cornish Class 37s had the last three digits of their running number shown on the cab ends. *Author*

Below: With a dozen bogie vans in tow Mainline-liveried No 47565, from the RXLC Crewe Class 47 locomotive pool of the Rail express systems Sector, is framed by the road overbridge as it powers through Liskeard station with the 21.56 Leeds to Penzance vans of 8 June 1990. Even at this late date the main line still comprised old bullhead rail. *Author*

Above: With the benefit of a lineside pass it was worth staying out late to photograph the Penzance to Paddington sleepers, especially when a truly immaculate No 47484 *Isambard Kingdom Brunel* arrived at the business end. Seen at Liskeard at 00.16 on 7 April 1990, the 22.45 ex-Penzance will soon disappear into the night aided by the visibly piercing headlight. The three vehicles nearest the loco are sleepers and the rest of the train is for the 'wakers'. *Author*

Middle: In days gone by there was a goods yard at both the up and down ends of Liskeard's up platform, as well as storage sidings on the down side behind the signalbox, where until 1918 a small engine shed was located. Shunting the Moorswater goods onto the main line on 24 June 1955 was 'Small Prairie' No 4523, with a rake of china clay wagons immediately behind the locomotive. Note the water tower at the up platform end. *R. E. Vincent*

Below: This 1950s panorama of the west or down end of Liskeard is full of interest. A small '45xx' class 2-6-2T is about to shunt forward before using the left-hand crossover to access the up goods yard. The yard is well populated with goods wagons of the era and there is unloading activity at the dock in front of the large goods shed. All goods facilities were withdrawn in June 1981 and the lines on the right were all lifted. As a consequence the up platform was extended in 1984 and 2006. *R. C. Riley/Transport Treasury*

4

Liskeard to Bodmin Road

The main line from Liskeard drops away steeply at 1 in 59 towards Moorswater Viaduct. This magnificent structure is 954ft long and 147ft high but unfortunately Brunel's original structure lasted for only 22 years. The timber fans were supported by a dozen masonry piers, each featuring up to four Gothic arched openings. The vast structure spanned the East Looe river and carried the railway across its wide valley. The viaduct had early problems and two of the piers partially collapsed and had to be rebuilt. Brunel adopted somewhat different engineering principles at Moorswater, with the timber supports being arranged in a different configuration to the similar Liskeard and St Pinnock viaducts. Nevertheless the viaduct was ready by the 1859 opening date. The structure ran into problems, some say by trains running quickly down the steep gradients at either end and onto the viaduct and by the 1870s at least two of the piers needed to be strapped to provide support and prevent collapse. Under the overall control of Margary it was decided to build a replacement viaduct with eight huge piers with the capacity to accommodate two standard-gauge tracks. Sadly the resident engineer, H. G. Cole, was killed in October 1878 when a steam-powered travelling crane toppled over while lifting stone. On 25 February 1881, at a cost of just over £30,000, the viaduct was ready for service,

carrying at that time a single broad-gauge line. Today there is ample evidence of the old original piers, while on the valley floor the freight line to Moorswater survives, although for cement traffic rather than the time-honoured china clay. Whether seen from the A38 Liskeard bypass or the area around Coombe Junction, Moorswater Viaduct is hugely impressive.

The line climbs steeply and curves its way up to Dobwalls and past Tremabe, where there was an up wartime goods loop that was not closed until 1952, then on to the site of Doublebois station. This section of line was doubled in February 1894. Doublebois station was opened a little later than the CR main line, opening its doors in June 1860. There was an up and a down platform with initially a passing loop between the platforms before the line was doubled. Once doubled, a signalbox was opened halfway along the up platform. At this

With rain giving way to sunshine, one of the handsome and glorious-sounding 'Western' Class 52 2,700hp C-C diesel hydraulics arrives at Liskeard on 15 May 1976. No D1028 *Western Hussar* was allocated to the 15.15 Penzance to Birmingham New Street. Note the engineers rail vehicles in the sidings, once part of the up side goods yard. *Author*

Whereas shining green *Isambard Kingdom Brunel* was the pride of the WR Class 47 fleet, green-liveried *Sir Edward Elgar* was distinctive, indeed unique, within the Region's fleet of Class 50s. With another soapy windscreen wash in progress, No 50007 leaves Liskeard on 11 June 1987 with the short-lived 05.45 Barnstaple to Penzance. *Author*

time there were eight staff. Eventually there were sidings to the east and the west of the station, all on the down side. The sidings at the eastern end were used by the military from 1943, with ammunition being the primary commodity handled, and later as a permanent way yard while those to the west comprised the original 1860 goods yard featuring a two-ton crane and cattle pens. All of these connections were taken out of use in January 1968, more than three years after the closure of the station in October 1964 and the withdrawal of freight two months later. Today nothing is left of the old station. Beyond Doublebois station the line descends sharply through the Glynn Valley of the River Fowey for over six miles with gradients as steep as 1 in 57. The line runs through miles of rhododendrons and Forestry Commission conifer plantations and passes over eight viaducts. The views to the north of the line are magnificent.

The first of the viaducts encountered is Westwood at 372ft in length and 88ft in height. The original viaduct was replaced in 1879 and in 1893, over a year after abolition of the broad gauge, the line from Doublebois to Bodmin Road was doubled. Just beyond Westwood Viaduct on the down side a siding served Westwood Quarry, which supplied much of the stone used for rebuilding the viaducts in the area in Victorian times. The very last old CR signalbox left standing was at Westwood, which after closure in 1879 was used as a permanent way hut, before becoming derelict and eventually being demolished some 90

years later. The next viaduct down the valley is St Pinnock, the highest in the entire county at a height of 151ft and a length of 633ft. It was built on nine fully buttressed piers with Gothic openings and, as with Liskeard Viaduct, instead of a new viaduct replacing the old timber-topped structure, in 1882 the piers were extended but in this case in masonry rather than brick. Much of the original metalwork was retained but in 1964 a decision was made to single the track across St Pinnock and Largin Viaducts to save the cost of expensive strengthening and renewals. This short section of single track remains and until 1991 movements were controlled by the 1906-built Largin signalbox. There was no water supply to the remote signalbox and water containers had to be dropped off from down trains. Below St Pinnock is the vast Trago Mills retail outlet, which looks somewhat incongruous amongst the forestry and in an area of outstanding natural beauty. Largin Viaduct, just 29 chains beyond St Pinnock, is another impressive structure 567ft long and 130ft high, which was partly replaced in 1886. Built on eight masonry piers with Gothic openings the viaduct was curved and yet again masonry extensions were provided to support girders that replaced the old wooden fan top.

The next viaducts in our run along the main line through Cornwall are West Largin, 315ft long and 75ft high, Draw Wood, 669ft long and 42ft high and Derrycombe, 369ft long and 77ft high. All three original viaducts were replaced by entirely new masonry structures capable of accommodating standard gauge double track. Rebuilding was completed and the new viaducts brought into use in 1875, 1875 and 1881 respectively. Clinnick Viaduct was originally built on three masonry piers but its 1879 replacement had six piers and six semicircular arches with decorative stone, resulting in a somewhat different-looking structure compared with others in the area. At 330ft in length and 74ft in height it carries the railway over a minor tributary of the River Fowey. The last viaduct before reaching Bodmin Road is Penadlake, 426ft long and 42ft in height. The original structure was all timber and built on a curve with a radius of about 2,000ft. Ten sets of double timber fans radiated from low masonry plinths. It was replaced by the present masonry structure in 1877 at a cost of less than £4,500. Beyond Panadlake on the down side was Onslow siding, originally laid down in the 1870s. It was then known as Glynn Valley siding and served a clay drying works. In 1933 a full goods loop was provided, which served Bowater Newbridge Clay Driers, controlled by Onslow signalbox on the opposite, or up side of the line. Both were closed in 1968.

The line continues to curve its way down to Bodmin Road station, known for the past quarter of a century as Bodmin Parkway, located over three miles from the town it purports to serve. The station opened on 26 June 1859, marginally later than the main line. For financial reasons the Cornwall Railway was unable to route its main line nearer to the town of Bodmin due to the surrounding topography. It was not until 1887 that a steeply-graded standard gauge branch line to the town of Bodmin was opened by the GWR, although the Bodmin and Wadebridge Railway had arrived in the town at what was to become Bodmin North as early as 1834. Due to the change of gauge there was no physical connection between the branch and

the main line at Bodmin Road until October 1892, five months after the abolition of the broad gauge main line. From 1893, when the line up to Doublebois and down to Lostwithiel was doubled, a signalbox was located halfway along the down platform. The box closed in November 1983 after the Wenford Bridge goods line, which ran via the then closed Bodmin General station, was closed to all traffic and all signals were removed. The two platforms are linked by a splendid covered overbridge with public road access only possible from the down side. The down platform was greatly lengthened in 1896 and to the west there was a down side goods yard with a substantial goods shed. There was also a private siding used by the English China Clays company from 1920 until 1966. This entire area now comprises the station car park, where the 'Parkway' label particularly applies. On the up side there was another goods yard with exchange sidings for traffic travelling to and from Bodmin General and beyond. There was also a long goods platform with awning, which was removed many years ago. The sidings were taken over by the Bodmin & Wenford Railway preservationists and in 2007 a large carriage shed was erected. There was once an unusual water column for steam engine replenishment at the up end of the up platform that straddled the branch connection, the track finally being removed in 1985. The branch platform became disused in January 1967 when passenger services to Bodmin General and beyond were withdrawn. However it is now again in use by the B&WR, with steam and diesel hauled trains taking passengers to Bodmin General and on to Boscarne Junction during the season. It should be added that new station buildings replaced the old ones on the up and down side during 1989 and the signalbox is now used as a café.

Moorswater Viaduct is impressive not only because of its size but due to its visibility from all directions. The current viaduct is an 1881 rebuild of the original, which lasted for only 22 years. At precisely 18.50 on a splendid 14 June 1989 Class 47/4 No 47652, in 'large logo' livery, heads the long distance 06.55 Glasgow and Edinburgh to Penzance InterCity express over the 147ft high structure. *Author*

Right: **This delightful little engraving came from Meason's 1860 *Official Illustrated Guide for Cornwall* and shows an impression of a train of the era crossing the original timber fan Moorswater Viaduct. Note the Gothic apertures in the piers, some of which survive today (see picture showing No 60082 *Mam Tor*).** *Cornish Studies Library*

Below: **With a 200mm Nikkor lens providing the impact, 3,100hp Class 60 No 60082 *Mam Tor* in Transrail livery hauls 990 tons of china clay slurry across Moorswater Viaduct on its way to Irvine in Scotland, on 22 June 1996. After 18 years of operation the 'Silver Bullet' ceased as a dedicated trainload, in January 2008. On the left are two of the original 1859 piers clearly showing their Gothic apertures.** *Author*

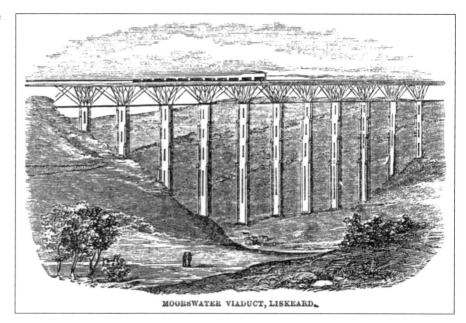

MOORSWATER VIADUCT, LISKEARD.

Above: **On a wonderful Cornish evening the returning 'Penzance Flyer' 'chartex', 1Z22, the 17.22 Penzance to Birmingham New Street, crosses a warmly lit Moorswater Viaduct headed by exciting and unusual motive power for Cornwall in the shape of two 'Dutch'-liveried Class 33s, Nos 33019 and 33002. The pair of 'Cromptons' were going well when photographed on 22 June 1996.** *Author*

Middle: **Moorswater Viaduct is approached in both directions on quite steep gradients, 1 in 61 in the up direction and 1 in 59 on the down. It is believed that the stress caused by trains travelling down these gradients and onto the viaduct at speed was one of the reasons for the failure of the first viaduct. Climbing away from Moorswater Viaduct on 4 April 1990 with loaded CDAs, weighing some 700 tonnes, is No 37670, which is initially bound for Lostwithiel.** *Author*

Left: **For some enthusiasts a photograph of an immaculate Railfreight Class 37 passing Dobwalls on CDA wagons will be as nostalgic as a 'Grange' class 4-6-0 steam locomotive passing the same spot with a vacuum braked freight. There is a saying that 'today's news is tomorrow's history' and certainly No 37671 *Tre Pol and Pen* descending towards Moorswater on 14 June 1989 is now a part of Cornwall's railway history.** *Author*

Above: **Nearing the summit of the climb up from Bodmin Road on a miserable and wet 2 October 1987 is all-blue No 47556 with the 12.10 Penzance to Glasgow vans. Looking at the redundant wooden sleepers and the apparently new flat-bottomed track, there has recently been some engineering works in the area. Also of interest is the freight and passenger train speed restriction signs just west of Doublebois station.** *Author*

Middle: **Back in 1961 this abandoned signal cabin was a remarkable survivor that dated back to the days of the CR. The signalbox was located at Westwood siding in the Glynn Valley, west of Doublebois and until closed in 1879 it controlled a broad gauge siding to Westwood Quarry, where stone for the replacement viaducts was quarried. After decades of use as a permanent way hut the little building was demolished in the 1960s.** *Maurice Dart*

Below: **This vintage view features Doublebois station in 1947. Looking towards Liskeard a local pick-up goods has come to a halt at the up platform as the locomotive pulls forward into the distance, while the shunter is seen beside the penultimate wagon. The station opened in 1860 and it was closed in October 1964, with the last goods train calling just two months later. There is now no trace of the station or the former sidings.** *Author's collection*

Left: This photograph features the main 1860 goods yard at Doublebois on the down side of the station, beyond an adjacent road bridge. The yard had a two-ton crane and cattle pens, which can be seen centre left. The main line descends towards Bodmin Road and a 'pin down the brakes' notice is just visible on the down road. Although undated, it would appear that this view also dates back to about 1947. *Author's Collection*

Middle: Giving its all on the climb up the Glynn Valley, opposite the road junction to Mount village, is No 6911 *Holker Hall* powering the 10.20am Penzance to Swansea towards Largin and Doublebois on 4 July 1959. The 'Halls' and the 'Granges' were the mainstay of GWR/WR motive power on the Cornish main line for some three decades but by this time their days were numbered. *Peter Gray*

Below: Just a few yards further west, on 20 May 1976, 2,700hp 'Western' Class 52 No D1041 *Western Prince* was making music in the hills as its two 12-cylinder Maybach engines were at maximum power with the early evening St Blazey to Stoke-on-Trent freight. Within nine months the entire Class 52 fleet of 74 locomotives would be extinct but this particular locomotive was fortunately preserved. *Author*

Above: **The unsung heroes of Cornish railway operations from the late-1960s until the mid-1980s were the heavy 1Co-Co1 Class 45 and 46 'Peak' locomotives. Eventually Plymouth Laira would have an allocation of Class 46s but in passenger train terms the classes were always associated with long-distance inter-regional trains. On 2 April 1979 No 46028 descends the Glynn Valley with the down Leeds to Penzance 'Cornishman'.** *Author*

Middle: **In previous years No 50040, originally *Leviathan* but renamed *Centurion* (a name previously carried by No 50011) in 1987, would have been crossing St Pinnock Viaduct on a Class 1 express passenger train but by 14 June 1989 it was allocated to humble Class 8 engineers ballast trains. The train of 'Dogfish' wagons was working from Lostwithiel to Tavistock Junction.** *Author*

Below: **Photographed from the A390 Dobwalls to Lostwithiel road through a powerful 300mm Nikkor lens, No 37673 in new Railfreight livery powers CDA clay wagons from Carne Point to Tavistock Junction across St Pinnock Viaduct on 17 March 1989. The track across the viaduct was singled in 1964 to avoid the cost of significant viaduct strengthening. On the right is a warehouse forming part of the Trago Mills complex.** *Author*

Left: With a trace of exhaust from its 2,500hp Sulzer engine, which is providing power for its Crompton Parkinson generator and traction motors, No 45006 *Honourable Artillery Company* is seen on full power as it crosses the 74ft-high Clinnick Viaduct on its climb to Doublebois with the 13.59 Penzance to Bristol Temple Meads, on 2 April 1979. *Author*

Below: Back in the 1960s a railway photographer in the Glynn Valley did not have to worry about the encroaching lineside foliage but gradually most of the fine photographic locations were completely obliterated from this scenic stretch of line. Heading the 9.20am from Falmouth across Clinnick Viaduct is 1,100hp North British Type 2 No D6325 on 26 April 1962. Note the white headcode discs, a leftover from the age of steam. *J. C. Beckett*

Above: **A magnificent photograph from the early days of the diesel-hydraulic revolution finds the prestigious 'Cornish Riviera Express' curving its way across Clinnick Viaduct and up the valley of the River Fowey between Bodmin Road and Liskeard, on 26 April 1962. The sound of the locomotive's two high-revving 1100hp Maybach engines will be reverberating against the hillside as No D809 *Champion* tackles gradients as steep as 1 in 57 for several miles. Note the splendid headboard and again, the white express passenger headcode discs.** *J. C. Beckett*

Below: **Another of the nine viaducts between Bodmin Road and Liskeard is Derrycombe, 369ft long and 77ft high. Descending the Glynn Valley on 21 April 1954 at milepost 271 (from Paddington via Bristol) is 'Grange' class 4-6-0 No 6817 *Gwenddwr Grange*. The locomotives had 5ft 8in driving wheels, over 12 inches less than a 'Castle' and some 4 inches less than a 'Hall', which resulted in them being ideal performers for the undulating, curving and speed-restricted Cornish main line.** *B. A. Butt*

Above: In stepping back from the railway line the photographer has recorded the delightful scenery in this part of the Glynn Valley. Drifting down towards Bodmin Road and crossing Penadlake Viaduct on 5 June 1961 is one of Collett's mixed-traffic 5MT 'Grange' class 4-6-0s with a mixed freight. *J. C. Beckett*

Below: Although located over three miles from the town of Bodmin, Bodmin Road (now Parkway) station is set in an idyllic, if isolated, location. From 1887 the town was connected to the GWR main line when a standard-gauge branch line was opened. Getting into its stride upon departure from Bodmin Road is No 50026 *Indomitable* with the nine-coach 07.40 Penzance to Liverpool on 3 June 1981. *Author*

Above: **A sight that many thought they would never see, a 'King' class 4-6-0 in Cornwall. Throughout their working lives from 1927 until withdrawn in the early 1960s the class were not permitted across the Royal Albert Bridge due to their restricted route availability (although there were a couple of reported but not photographed incursions). However, following bridge strengthening, one of the GWR's finest finally penetrated the Royal Duchy. Blasting through Bodmin Parkway on 28 October 2006 is No 6024 *King Edward I* with the return leg of 'The Cornubian' railtour. Sharing the limelight is veteran LSWR Beattie Class 0298 well tank No 30585, working on the Bodmin & Wenford Railway.** *J. C. Beckett*

Middle: **This fine view of Bodmin Road, looking west towards Lostwithiel, dates back to 1922. In addition to the up and down main lines there are lines on the right, the island platform road mostly being used by Bodmin General branch trains. Note that the up starting signal is on the down side and the locomotive watering system is something of a novelty. The water supply came from the River Fowey, located just below the water tank on the right.** *Ian Allan Library*

Right: **In this fascinating scene there are goods yards on both the up and down side at the western end of Bodmin Road station. There were once fine goods sheds in both yards but the area on the left is now the station car park, while on the right the Bodmin & Wenford Railway erected a carriage shed over the old sidings during 2007. To the right of the down starting lower quadrant signal is the Bodmin General (and Wadebridge) branch line. 'Hall' class No 5925 *Eastcote Hall* is seen arriving with an up train.** *Author's Collection*

Left: One can almost hear the staccato blast of two-cylinder 'Hall' class 4-6-0 No 4908 *Broom Hall* restarting the down 'Cornishman' on 11 June 1956. The chocolate and cream BR Mk 1 coaches had just been introduced on this train and the named 'Cornish Riviera' and 'Royal Duchy' expresses. The copper-topped chimney and safety valve covers were always associated with GWR locomotives. *Michael Mensing*

Middle: By September 2003, nearly half a century later, the contrast between trains could not be greater. Rather than a smoke-belching, smut-producing but nevertheless evocative steam locomotive, a pair of streamlined air-conditioned 125mph diesel units in the shape of two Virgin Voyagers have appeared on the down main line at Bodmin Parkway. Note the weed-infested track, resembling some little used rural branch line. Thankfully the fine pedestrian overbridge graces both scenes. *Author*

Bottom: The residents of Bodmin had to wait until 1887 before their town was linked with the GWR main line, although the town had been served from the Wadebridge direction, albeit with no rail connection to the 'outside world', from 1834. However, by January 1967 the branch was struggling to make a profit and under the influence of the by then departed Dr Beeching the branch was closed to passengers. Seen from the weed-covered sidings No 47656 produces a cloud of exhaust on 17 June 1989 as it departs from Bodmin Parkway with the 07.50 Glasgow to Penzance. *Author*

Above: **By the start of the 1960s railway photographers were recording the remaining but numerically declining steam locomotives but few pointed their cameras in the direction of the new green diesel mechanical units with 'whiskers' on the cab ends. There are six railway staff but no passengers visible in this view of Plymouth to Penzance local 2C70, on 2 May 1961. The wonderful running-in board shows the travel potential by changing at Bodmin Road!** *R. C. Riley/Transport Treasury*

Below: **Although photographed as recently as 15 April 1981, this photograph shows another piece of modern traction history in the making at Bodmin Road. Grubby Class 37 No 37232 is shunting the up goods yard, which was still being used for wagon storage and marshalling, while on the left No 37142 powers china clay hoods up the gradient and through the station with the 18.10 St Blazey to Tavistock Junction freight. Coincidentally the latter locomotive was subsequently preserved on the adjacent Bodmin & Wenford Railway.** *Author*

5

Bodmin Road to Lostwithiel

From Bodmin Road the line continues to descend, initially at 1 in 65, towards Respryn Bridge where a road bridge crosses the line. Just north of the railway the same road crosses the medieval multi-arched Respryn Bridge over the River Fowey. There was once a small temporary private station at Respryn serving nearby Lanhydrock House, which was open only between 3 May and 26 June 1859. On a wide sweep the line approaches the 88 yard Brownqueen Tunnel, 275 miles from London via Bristol. The line follows the course of the valley but in the process turns through 90 degrees to face south east at one point, while travelling west! The line passes the elevated ancient ruins of Restormel Castle and through Lostwithiel golf course before reaching a four-track section that includes both up and down goods loops, all controlled by lower quadrant semaphore signals. Before arriving at Lostwithiel station there was once a flourishing milk depot and additional sidings on the up side, which from 1932 were used to load milk tank wagons that were destined for London. The traffic ceased about 1980. Also on the up side was a substantial loading dock. Such is the curvature of the line that Lostwithiel station is located on a north/south axis. The river at this point was once navigable and between 1836 and 1883 there was a riverside quay where iron ore was loaded on to vessels. There remains evidence of former river traffic in the shape of a limekiln on the west side of the river, just down the road from the excellent Lostwithiel bakery. During the building of the CR rails and timbers were landed at Lostwithiel.

There is a busy level crossing at the station, which is controlled by the 1893 Lostwithiel signalbox, with the signalman raising and lowering the barriers as necessary. This is an ancient site in terms of railway history and the main Cornwall Railway's wagon and carriage works were located at the down end of the up platform. From 1869 the station was the junction for Fowey but a passenger service did not commence until 1895 and was withdrawn in 1965. At the former date there were substantial changes made to the infrastructure with a third platform face provided for branch trains, station canopies constructed, a footbridge installed plus of course many changes in track layout. Beyond the down platform there is a series of weed covered sidings that were mostly used for berthing and marshalling china clay trains destined for and returning from Carne Point at Fowey. Beyond these a branch signalbox was in operation from 1895 until 1923. There was a large goods shed on the up side that dated back to the days of the broad gauge but which was, sadly, dismantled in October 1982. Goods

Pacific 4-6-2 steam locomotives were a rarity in Cornwall but during the early 1950s a handful of BR's 'Britannias' worked some of the county's most prestigious express trains. Here the up 'Cornishman', the 10.35am ex-Penzance, runs between Lostwithiel and Bodmin Road on 25 June 1955 behind No 70016 *Ariel*. Built at Derby from 1951, the locomotives weighed more than a 'King' class 4-6-0 but the 'Britannias' carried their weight on six axles rather than five. *R. E. Vincent*

facilities were withdrawn from June 1964, although clay wagons can still be found in the area. The old works building remained part derelict and part in commercial use but a major redevelopment occurred from 2004 when the buildings were incorporated in a new complex of apartments and town houses. The lovely old Victorian station buildings at Lostwithiel were demolished in 1976 (down side) and 1981 (up side) and replaced by a small but tasteful up side station building and a quite awful stone and concrete shelter on the down platform.

The passenger footbridge had been removed some years earlier. The station booking office is manned part time and locked at other times, a situation far removed from the 14 employees that were on hand in GWR days. The station is a great place to observe train movements, as they slow for the curve through the platforms under the control of lower-quadrant semaphore signals, which together with the crossing barriers give ample warning of an approaching train.

Right: **This view from Meason's 1860 *Illustrated Guide of Cornwall* shows an impression of a broad-gauge train making for Lostwithiel, below the remains of Restormel Castle. The site is now a golf course but the manor house centre right survives to this day.**
Cornish Studies Library

Below: **Continuing down from Bodmin Parkway the line passes Respryn Bridge and encounters the short 88-yard Brownqueen Tunnel. On 8 May 1976 No 47031 bursts out of the tunnel with a down express. The train headcode has been turned to '0000' because in January of that year the practice of showing four-digit train identifying numbers on the roller blinds of locomotives ceased. Nearly all such panels were eventually plated over and marker lights fitted.** *H. T. Heyl*

RESTORMEL CASTLE, NEAR LOSTWITHIEL.

Above: **Respryn Bridge, named after the ancient road bridge that crosses the River Fowey just north of this location, is a great place to observe trains except that on sunny days up trains are best photographed in the morning and down trains in the late afternoon. This Class 37, thought to be No 37521, is in the latter category as it heads west with the weekly Tavistock Junction to Ponsandane fuel tankers.** *Author*

Below: **Exceedingly rare power, especially in this formation, is featured here passing Respryn Bridge on 4 June 2006 in the shape of GBRf Class 66s Nos 66715 *Valour* and 66703 *Doncaster PSB*, heading train 6G50, a Westbury to St Blazey engineers rail train. If the train had been any later the dark shadows would have 'crossed the line' and obscured these amazing interlopers.** *Sam Felce*

Above: **This is the view from the opposite or down side of the road bridge at Respryn, which is adjacent to the grounds of the nearby Lanhydrock House. Setting a cracking pace with the 11.15 Newquay to Wolverhampton Low Level of 6 July 1955 is No 1006 *County of Cornwall*, one of Hawksworth's 1945-built high-pressure two-cylinder 4-6-0s. Of particular note is the meticulously tamed condition of the lineside vegetation.** *R. C. Riley/Transport Treasury*

Below: **Some 40 years later, on 25 September 1994, a pair of truly immaculate Transrail Class 37s are applying to the rail over three times the power of the 'County' class 4-6-0 as they approach Respryn Bridge with the 11.05 Burngullow to Irvine china clay slurry train. However, this train will weigh 1,000 tonnes, compared with little more than 200 tonnes above. The locomotives are No 37695 and 37412 *Driver John Elliott*. Note the appalling state of the lineside maintenance compared with 1955.** *Author*

Above: **Before the growth of lineside foliage this was one of the finest panoramas on the Cornish main line, overlooking what was then a very new Lostwithiel golf course. The town of Lostwithiel can be seen in the left background, while just out of frame on the right are the ruins of Restormel Castle. A full length InterCity 125 unit makes for Paddington from Penzance in August 1994.** *Author*

Below: **This perspective at Lostwithiel shows the alignment of the main line in the context of the course of the River Fowey. With the Cornwall River Authority water level measure in the foreground and a farm bridge on the left, a westbound IC125 passes along the valley in the shadow of Restormel Castle during the summer of 1994.** *Author*

Right: As late as the 1980s an observer spending a day beside the Cornish main line would be rewarded with a succession of van trains and for many years a regular was the 13.50 Penzance to Bristol postal. No 47574 *Benjamin Gimbert G.C.* looks attractive in large logo blue livery with wrap round yellow ends and a black former headcode panel as it sweeps past Restormel on the up road, on 15 June 1989. *Author*

Middle: There is thunder in the valley as the driver of Nos 37141 and 37142 opens the taps to unleash 3,500hp of English Electric power to maintain the momentum of the 17.00 St Blazey to Exeter Riverside air-braked freight of 21 September 1994. The locomotives are both in Civil Engineers 'Dutch' livery and much of the train comprises china clay in liquid, or slurry, form. *Author*

Below: A view that shows modern trains but vintage signalling, on the approach to Lostwithiel. General Motors Class 66s first worked china clay trains in Cornwall at the end of 1999 but eventually they replaced the ageing Class 37s. No 66229 is held at signals in the down freight loop as this First Great Western IC125 from Paddington to Penzance passes at line speed. From 1979 IC125 units gradually replaced locomotive-hauled main-line passenger trains. *Author*

Left: Headed by a grimy work-stained 16-wheeled No 45043 *The King's Own Royal Border Regiment*, this ex-St Blazey up freight is slowly gathering speed just to the east of Lostwithiel. These 'Peak' class locomotives were banned from working west of Bristol from October 1985, bringing to an end some 16 years of operation in the south west. Note the remains of Restormel Castle on the hill above the locomotive. *Author*

Above: There are few finer sights than a gleaming four-cylinder 'Castle', even if it is attached to one of the less attractive straight-sided tenders. Approaching Lostwithiel with a morning down express from Paddington is No 4077 *Chepstow Castle*, on 10 July 1955. Note the up and down goods loops and, the distant water tower. *R. C. Riley/Transport Treasury*

Left: The approach to Lostwithiel on 17 June 1989. A most interesting train is entering the frame, the overnight 22.00 Glasgow to Penzance sleepers, headed by 'generator' Class 47 No 47403 in Mainline (unbranded InterCity) livery. Note that the third to the sixth vehicles are all sleeping cars. By the end of the 1980s most main-line diesel locomotives had been fitted with headlights. *Author*

Above: **Another 'past and present' comparison featuring the up end of Lostwithiel station. Rounding the curve on the up main is 'Hall' class 4-6-0 No 5915 *Trentham Hall*, seen here passing the dairy where an entire range of milk products were produced. Of particular interest is the siding containing a number of 3,000-gallon six-wheeled milk tankers that made their way to and from London on a daily basis.** *R. C. Riley/Transport Treasury*

Middle: **By October 1991 the milk depot had grown out of all recognition but ironically not one drop of the substance left the Lostwithiel establishment by rail! The total infrastructure has changed so much so that the only common points of reference are the railway line itself and the line of the hedgerows in the very top left of the scene. In red and grey parcels livery a resplendent No 47634 *Holbeck* of the RXLC pool heads the 12.12 Penzance to Paddington vans.** *Author*

Right: **With the Class 50s very much in the twilight of their lives some of the less-fit locomotives were relegated to the trains of the Civil Engineer. Such was the case in June 1989 when No 50040 *Centurion* (originally *Leviathan*) was employed on a ballast train, which was unusually stabled in the down loop at Lostwithiel. Passing by at speed are 2,250hp power cars Nos 43011 and 43024 with the 08.26 Penzance to Paddington.** *Author*

Above: **The palm trees at Lostwithiel station give this scene a Mediterranean (or at least a 'Riviera') feel. Sadly the photograph shows the demise of the lovely old wooden Victorian station building on the down platform, which in May 1976, was in the process of being demolished. The up building would last a little longer but was in urgent need of maintenance. Swindon three-car cross-country Class 120 DMU unit No P555 departs with a local from Plymouth to Par.** *Author*

Middle: **Here the modern version of the single power car diesel unit arrives at Lostwithiel in September 2004. The Class 153 unit, No 153374, is operating one of the through workings from Plymouth to Newquay, which will leave the main line at Par. It should be noted that the down station building has been replaced by this miserable, featureless and comfort-free stone hut.** *Author*

Left: **In what amounts to a Class 37 convention, locomotives sporting three different liveries line up at Lostwithiel in October 1993. On the left DCWA pool No 37207 in 'Dutch' livery heads 11 ex-Dover Polybulks, which have returned from Italy, while on the right the second half of the 22-Polybulk train waits in the down loop behind Mainline-liveried No 37416 and new Railfreight No 37674.** *Author*

Right: After a long wait in the down loop the double-headed down empty Polybulks were given the right away by the Lostwithiel signalman and Nos 37416 and 37674 are seen powering through the station in an attempt to gain momentum for the climb up to Treverrin Tunnel. The up starting lower quadrant semaphore signal, complete with finial, is a feature as some CDA clay wagons lurk in the background. *Author*

Below: This photograph demonstrates the longevity of the service given to the Cornish main line by the 'Hall' class 4-6-0s. Arriving at Lostwithiel with a down train and passing the 1893-dated signalbox, on 22 May 1935 is No 4907 *Broughton Hall*. The 1895 pedestrian overbridge was demolished in the early 1960s. Note the 'Change for Fowey' addition to the Lostwithiel running in board. *H. C. Casserley/Maurice Dart Collection*

Left: Thought to have been taken in 1922, this photograph of Lostwithiel station shows the footbridge to advantage. Seen from the up end, there is activity at the station as an 0-6-0 pannier tank toys with a wagon during shunting operations, while the shunter, with pole, is waiting on the down platform. The station platform lamps are a sheer delight. *Cornish Studies Library*

Middle: No 6397, one of the handsome GWR '43xx' class moguls, drifts into Lostwithiel on 14 August 1958 with an up local. The original up side broad gauge goods shed is on the right and there seems to be a healthy number of freight wagons in the headshunt. To the right of the train is an elevated banner repeating signal and on the left a wooden-post semaphore, down side locomotive water column and some wooden-bodied china clay wagons. *Norman Simmons/Maurice Dart Collection*

Below: The branch passenger service to Fowey started in 1895 but by 1965 closure was on the cards. Looking very much like a scene from *The Titfield Thunderbolt*, 0-4-2T No 1408 and its train crew pose for the camera on 11 June 1956, before departing from the down bay platform with the 5.5pm branch auto train. Note the GWR station seat. *Michael Mensing*

Right: The idea behind this 1993 photograph was to compare ancient with modern but such is the pace of progress on the railways that the modern has now become 'ancient'! A Class 156 Super Sprinter unit heads west at Lostwithiel as seen through the remains of the original old CR works. The old buildings and the surrounding site were redeveloped with new town houses and apartments while the Class 156s were transferred off-region after a short stay. *Author*

Right: Throughout the 1970s and the early 1980s the old Lostwithiel goods shed regularly provided shelter for the railway photographer during the seemingly endless bouts of inclement weather. On such a day in 1977 up and down trains of clay hoods were hauled by all-blue Class 47s, with the up train about to be held at signals. *Author*

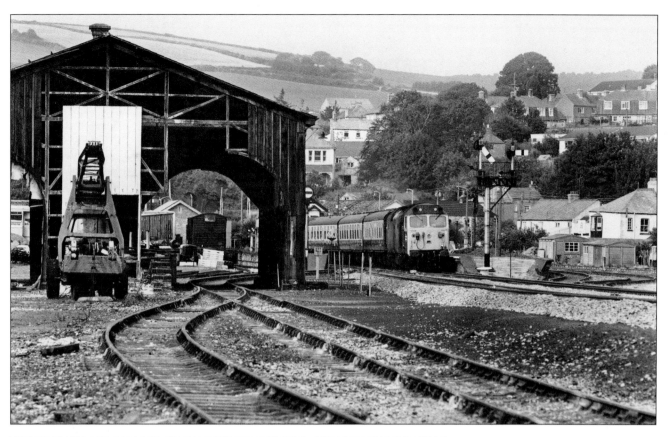

Above: The end was nigh for the old broad-gauge goods shed at Lostwithiel on 22 July 1982. The shed was dismantled plank by plank with a view to reassembly and preservation but the purchaser's plans did not come to fruition and some reports suggested that the whole thing had been incinerated. Passing the sad scene is No 50013 *Agincourt* with a Plymouth to Penzance local. *Author*

Middle: With new apartments on the site of the old CR works on the right, a beautifully presented five-car Voyager operated by Virgin Trains glides past the semaphores towards Lostwithiel station in October 2007, with the 09.30 Penzance to Glasgow. It seems a shame that such a fine-looking unit has so many shortcomings in terms of internal seating layout and passenger space, at least for those travelling standard class. *Author*

Bottom: One of the most appropriate names ever applied to a locomotive in Cornwall was when No 37521 was named *English China Clays*, a company that had contributed millions of pounds to BR and the new English Welsh & Scottish Railway company. The immaculate locomotive in the EWS red and gold livery leaves Lostwithiel in the down direction in August 1997. Few would have anticipated that the long-established ECC company would soon be taken over by a French corporation! *Author*

6

Lostwithiel to Par

The line climbs away from the ancient town of Lostwithiel at about 1 in 70 and crosses the River Fowey. Until 1972 the Fowey branch line had its own track and girder bridge across the river but from that time branch trains have used the down main line to access the branch. Conversely empty china clay trains from Carne Point run up to the goods loops along the down main line, which is slightly worrying when observing train movements from the platforms, even though all movements are of course under the control of the signalman. As the main line and the branch separate, the main line route curves its way up to Milltown Viaduct, 501ft long and 75ft high. The original Margary Class A wooden-topped viaduct was not replaced until 1893, when a new masonry example was built, three years before the line from Par to Lostwithiel was doubled but after the abolition of the broad gauge. The line continues to climb quite steeply past the site of the long-closed Milltown Viaduct signalbox .

Treverrin signalbox was located on the up side just before the line plunged into the 565yard Treverrin Tunnel. The box was open from 1911 until 1956. Once through the notoriously wet tunnel the line descends past the old engine house at Wheal Treasure and road bridges at Stoneybridge and Treesmill, before reaching the outskirts of Par in the valley below Tywardreath. On the approach to Par there is a down goods loop, which opened in 1943. This is occasionally used for berthing china clay trains. There is a long curve on the approach to Par station, which is also located on a north/south axis, even though trains are eastbound or westbound. Par is the junction for Newquay, passengers changing trains and gauges between 1879, when a double track spur was built from the Cornwall Minerals Railway's Par station (later renamed St Blazey), and 1892 when the broad gauge was abolished. There is an up and a down main line platform and an island platform for branch line trains and down freights travelling to St Blazey yard (or by china clay workings to Rocks china clay works at Goonbarrow Junction on the Newquay branch). It is also possible to access the island platform from either the up or down main line, and for up freights there is an additional non-platform line that runs parallel with the island platform line before making a junction with the up main line. All movements are controlled by lower quadrant semaphore signals activated by the signalman in the 1890 signalbox located at the down end of the up platform. The box is now the oldest working example in Cornwall. There was much rebuilding in 1908 when, in particular, the down side station structure was enlarged. A new 57-lever frame was installed in the box in 1913 and a panel to control colour lights between Par and Probus, including St Austell and Burngullow, was squeezed into the box in 1985.

The island platform was also extended in 1913 and again in 1924. In the latter year there were 24 staff allocated to Par station. Occupying part of the main up goods yard area, which was abandoned in October 1964, is a Signalling and Telecommunications depot. A transshipment shed was once located at this site, where goods were transferred from standard to broad gauge wagons and vice versa. There was also a two-ton capacity crane available. In 1968 an up side siding was altered to accommodate Freightliner trains but no long-term contracts materialised and the idea fizzled out. To the south of the station on the up side a refuge and carriage siding is retained. Known as Chapel sidings, the line was often used by Newquay branch trains during layovers but more recently for the berthing of Rail Head Treatment Trains (RHTTs), especially in the autumn months when there are leaves on the lines. Although the structures on the up platform are modern, the lovely old granite station building on the down side remains. The passenger overbridge survives but without its original protective roof. There is no passenger access to the up main line or branch platforms except via the footbridge. Standing above the station is the Royal Inn, a useful watering hole when trains are late running! Par and Lostwithiel are the best places to watch trains in Cornwall in terms of frequency of movement, although even here there can be long gaps between trains.

Although outside the scope of this volume brief mention must be made of St Blazey depot that was opened by the CMR in 1874 at the same time as the Newquay branch line and the old abandoned direct line to Fowey were opened for freight traffic (passenger trains followed in 1876). The site is located within half a mile of the Par station complex but away from the main line. The first rails in the area were those of the horse and incline operated Treffry Tramway, which opened between Ponts Mill and some quarries above Luxulyan in 1841 and to Mollinis at Bugle in 1844. A canal was built between Par Harbour and Ponts Mill in 1838 but this was replaced by an extended tramway in 1855. Joseph Thomas Treffry constructed the tidal Par Harbour between 1828 and 1838, with the first commercial vessel calling in 1833. From that time the volume of minerals handled, mostly china clay, has increased out of all recognition. The harbour is still rail served by a direct single line from there to St Blazey. The main line crosses this track on a series of arches. St Blazey depot comprised many buildings with a nine-road semi-roundhouse, which was accessed via a turntable, being the primary feature. Since 1987 the Grade II listed building has been in light industrial use. Over the years there have been numerous changes in track layout and function but in 2008 the site was virtually abandoned as the EWS(now DB Schenker) freight company moved its operations to Carne Point, Fowey. The site is now used only for marshalling wagons, with china clay products dominating the scene. St Blazey signalbox controls all movements into and out of the yard and Newquay branch traffic.

Opposite: **There is much to absorb in this elevated view of the Lostwithiel station complex. In addition to No 50038 *Formidable* heading for Penzance with an inter-regional train, there is a Class 37 in the down freight loop, two long rakes of china clay wagons in the down sidings, the River Fowey just above the locomotive and the Fowey branch line bottom right.** *Author*

Above: **Making a truly wondrous sound from its 12-cylinder engine is 'large logo'-liveried No 37175 in April 1987, as it pounds up the 1 in 57/72 towards Treverrin Tunnel with a long train of empty clay hoods, all of which would be withdrawn ten months later. The town of Lostwithiel forms the backcloth on a glorious afternoon.** *Author*

Below: **Pounding up the climb to Treverrin is 'Castle' class No 4099 *Kilgerran Castle,* which was relegated to freight duty on 13 June 1956. The cattle wagons next to the engine were used primarily for loads of broccoli and other seasonal produce, which was loaded mainly at Marazion. Treverrin signalbox in the left background was about to close and a non-commissioned colour light on the right shares the space with a soon-to-be-abandoned semaphore.** *Michael Mensing*

Left: **A completely appropriate locomotive to be found on the Cornish main line was No 47625 *City of Truro*, seen here descending into Lostwithiel with an up InterCity working, on 4 April 1986. The Fowey branch can be seen below the Class 47 with the River Fowey at high tide below that. Ducks and boats complete the picture.** *Author*

Below: **Just below Treverrin Tunnel is the relatively inaccessible Milltown Viaduct, 501ft long and 75ft high, which replaced an earlier viaduct in 1893. Curving across the structure on the up road in April 1987 is No 47033 with the Mondays-only Truro to Ince UKF empty 'Shellstar' fertiliser wagons. On this day some additional freight wagons had been added to the train at St Blazey.** *Author*

Above: **This slightly unusual long shot shows a Paddington to Penzance IC125 leaving Treverrin Tunnel, in April 1990. The mouth of the notoriously wet 565-yard tunnel features prominently on the left of the photograph. Having breasted the summit the train will now descend at 1 in 62 to Par station, passing plenty of grazing sheep in the process.** *Author*

Middle: **In modern traction terms sights such as this are sorely missed, as locomotive-hauled trains have gradually been replaced by a variety of multiple-units on the Cornish main line. Descending between Stoneybridge and Treesmill, east of Par, on a beautiful April afternoon in 1986 is No 50023 *Howe* with the down Liverpool to Penzance express.** *Author*

Right: **Although empty, this single Class 37 heads a truly massive train of at least 34 CDA wagons, seen just west of Treverrin Tunnel in June 1989. No 37669 is in original Railfreight livery and the train will have originated at Carne Point, which is effectively Fowey Docks, Cornwall's primary export outlet for china clay products.** *Author*

Above: Normally the returning Irvine to Burngullow china clay slurry tankers travelled overnight, arriving back in Cornwall early in the morning. Accordingly the down working could only be photographed if running late. After a tip-off was received on 10 April 1990 a substantial 15-wagon load was captured on film climbing up to Treverrin Tunnel at 13.10, many hours behind schedule. Nos 37673 and 37414 are seen with the gleaming tankers comprising the 'Silver Bullet'. *Author*

Below: **Can you imagine the scene? On a fine April afternoon in 1986 and having been perched on a remote hillside for a couple of hours the rumble of a train is heard. You are set up for a down train but the train in Treverrin Tunnel is an up working. As the train emerges from the tunnel and with little warning there is a sudden realisation that the locomotive is immaculate and in green livery and the stock behind it is maroon. The Royal Train has just passed! In this 'grab' shot No 47500 *Great Western* finds a patch of sun as it heads a wonderful mixture of modern and vintage stock towards Lostwithiel.** *Author*

Above: In this quartet of photographs GWR/WR steam locomotives are featured, working hard to the east of Par. In this view the up Sunday 'Cornishman' is seen leaving Par behind 4-cylinder 'Castle' class 4-6-0 No 4077 *Chepstow Castle*, on 5 August 1956. The 'Castle' class replaced the 'Star' class 4-6-0s that had operated in the county since Edwardian times. *Les Elsey*

Below: The photographer barely had time to move his feet on 5 August 1956 when 'Hall' class No 6931 *Aldborough Hall* came into view and is seen here darkening the skies at Par with a through train from Newquay to Paddington. The second carriage is a restaurant car and the locomotive is one of Cornwall's own, being allocated to 83F, Truro. *Les Elsey*

Above: **Although only loaded to seven coaches, this view confirms the mixed-traffic capabilities of the GWR '43xx' class 2-6-0 moguls. No 5376 is entrusted to an express train in the shape of a Falmouth to Bradford working, which is seen approaching Treverrin Tunnel, at the summit of a two-mile climb at 1 in 62/64, also on 5 August 1956.** *Les Elsey*

Below: **Maintaining the variety of motive power on a summer's day on the Cornish main line is this illustration of passing 'County' class 4-6-0s. Crossing Milltown Viaduct with a down train on 9 July 1955 is No 1018 *County of Leicester* double-heading with a '43xx' class Mogul. On the up road another, unidentified, 'County' is about to cross its sister locomotive.** *R. C. Riley/Transport Treasury*

Above: **Seen from the top of a field at Tywardreath (pronounced tide-wreath) east of Par, the Penzance to Glasgow vans had loaded to 13 bogie vehicles on 3 April 1986. On this day the important train was entrusted to No 50027 *Lion*. From 1978 the Class 50s were all named after British warships but the 'Warship' label was never adopted by enthusiasts, who continued to associate the name with the earlier Class 41/42/43 'Warships'.** *Author*

Below: **Winter lighting has produced this backlit image, recorded at Treesmill in January 1988. A Class 47/3 is seen climbing away from Par with the 14.50 St Blazey to Gloucester air-braked freight. A sense of movement is enhanced by the exhaust trail from the Sulzer 2,580hp 12-cylinder diesel engine.** *Author*

Above: **During 2003, once postal trains working down to Plymouth and Penzance had been unloaded, they would travel empty to St Blazey depot for servicing. These movements produced a bonus for the railway photographer, until the contract between EWS and Royal Mail was terminated! Having run round its train in Par station No 67024 has propelled its stock along the up main line and is seen here pulling forward to gain access to St Blazey, in September 2003.** *Author*

Below: **The longevity of service of various types of railway motive power is relevant to the history of the Cornish main line. Over the years there has been the suggestion that because of the modernity and complexity of diesel locomotives there was no way in which they could compete with steam locomotive simplicity and durability. Other than for early pilot scheme diesels this has proved not to be the case and the Class 47s, for example, have been working in Cornwall for more than 40 years! In October 2007 two brightly painted yellow, orange and black Colas Rail Class 47s arrived in Cornwall to haul Railhead Treatment Trains and No 47749** *Demelza* **is seen here at Par.** *Author*

Right: This double-page spread shows diverse climatic conditions at the junction station of Par, one of the busiest in Cornwall. Although in recent years drainage has been improved Par station is low lying and susceptible to flooding. On 11 February 1974 this Class 52 'Western' heading the up 'Cornishman' was described as 'splashing' its way into the station; perhaps a good argument for hydraulic rather than electric transmission? *Ian Allan Library*

Below: An invitation into the 1890 Par signalbox was a real bonus on this wretched day when the heavens opened from dawn to dusk. Passing the soaking platforms with not a passenger or railman in sight is No 37274 with a Carne Point to Drinnick Mill train of empty clay hoods. Railfans positioned east of Lostwithiel or west of Burngullow would fail to see the majority of these local trip workings. *Author*

Left: Except on the heights of Bodmin Moor, snow is a fairly rare commodity in Cornwall but overnight on 19 January 1985 there were moderate falls, providing justification for a railway photographic safari. With the passengers no doubt tucked-up in their electrically-heated air-conditioned coaches, large logo No 50015 *Valiant* has just arrived at a snow-covered Par with the 07.30 Penzance to Glasgow. The Newquay branch DMU can be seen at the island platform. *Author*

Below: The expression 'raining cats and dogs' comes to mind as the poor old shunter has to brave the elements to uncouple No 37672 *Freight Transport Association* from IC125 power car No 43057 *Bounds Green*, after the 'Syphon' had helped the unit to and from Newquay, following the failure of one power car. The IC125 was able to continue its journey forward on one power car, the fearsome 1 in 37 climb up the Luxulyan Valley having been overcome on the way to Newquay. *Author*

Left: In contrast to the previous photograph this modern scene was recorded on a golden Cornish late-summer afternoon. Running through the station on the down main line, GM Class 66 No 66019 heads empty CDA wagons from Carne Point to Parkandillack on the Drinnick Mill branch. These powerful high-tech locomotives can haul 38 loaded CDAs, grossing to some 1,900 tonnes, unaided on the Cornish circuit, the downside for the railfan being far fewer trains. *Author*

Above: **Since the end of steam traction the local Newquay branch services have been in the hands of various types of diesel mechanical and diesel hydraulic units. For some 30 years the Pressed Steel Company Class 121 and Gloucester Class 122 single power cars were consistent performers but without having a monopoly. At busier times a pair of single cars would sometimes be coupled, as seen here at Par's island platform in April 1993.** *Author*

Below: **The old transfer goods shed was located in the up side goods yard on the north side of Par station. Once upon a time goods were transferred from standard gauge to broad gauge wagons. Sadly the shed was demolished as general goods services were withdrawn in October 1964. With the early British Railways legend on the side tanks 2-6-2 'Prairie' tank No 4526 simmers just outside the shed in about 1950.** *Cornish Studies Library*

Above: **This general view of Par station is believed to have been taken by local St Blazey photographer Dalby-Smith and dates back to Edwardian times. The up platform was extended in 1913 and again in 1924 and later still the old wooden station buildings were demolished and replaced by a shelter beyond the covered footbridge. The transfer goods shed, loading dock and cattle pens can be seen in the background, while a goods train occupies the up main line.** *Author's Collection*

Below: **This unique event occurred in February 1990 and the author was fortunate to be 'on the spot' with a camera. Class 56 No 56013 had been sent to the south west overnight for trials, with a view to replacing pairs of 1,750hp Class 37 locomotives with a single 3,250hp freight engine on long distance freights. Having worked CDA wagons to Lostwithiel, where it was looped, No 47815 rushed by on the down sleepers, which promptly failed on Treverrin bank. The Class 56 was sent a 'light engine' to assist and it is seen here having just propelled the train into Par station. After run round the Class 56 headed the failed Class 47 and the train to Penzance.** *Author*

7

Par to St Austell

For almost seven miles the main line climbs away from Par to Burngullow. The Par to St Austell section was doubled in October 1893. After passing the aforementioned Chapel sidings the main line crosses the Par Harbour branch and passes the harbour complex that is located on the down or south side. From 2008 all coastal shipping movements were concentrated on Fowey Docks. There are fine views of the harbour and the English Channel. There was a reverse connection made into the harbour area from the down main line but this closed in 1965, along with Par Harbour signalbox, also on the down side. On the up side are a series of abandoned china clay dries, all once part of the Par Moor complex. The main line crosses Carlyon Bay golf course but the cliffs above Carlyon Bay and the sea shore are out of sight. Climbing at 1 in 60 the main line reaches the suburbs of St Austell, for many years the administrative hub of the china clay industry by virtue of the headquarters building of the English China Clays Company, and also the home of the St Austell brewery.

Originally the 'second' St Austell goods yard was located on the down side of the station at the far western end of the platform but in 1931 it was moved some 30 chains to the east of the station, beyond a main road bridge. Also in 1931 a road crossing at the west end of the station was closed off and replaced by a pedestrian footbridge for use by the general public. At its peak there were seven sidings in the new goods yard, including a long single-road goods shed and a long loading dock. A five-ton crane was a useful facility. The goods yard was accessed via a single-line connection from an up goods loop adjacent to the main line, controlled by a ground frame. The yard was closed to general goods traffic in May 1968 but remained open for complete loads, such as coal, until 1985. The yard was also used by locomotives running round Motorail trains, which until 1984 ran to St Austell from Kensington Olympia. Since closure the entire track has been lifted. At the station site there were moderately-sized buildings on both the up and down sides, however the old, substantially wooden down side building was demolished in 1999 and a new modern version was opened in June 2000. For 120 years a splendid cast iron GWR pedestrian overbridge has connected the platforms but in 2008 the roof was in urgent need of attention! West of the station on the up side was the original CR goods yard that comprised a single track and a goods shed. The original signalbox was at the down end of the down platform, adjacent to the second goods yard (closed in 1931, as mentioned above). In Victorian times the main signalbox was built on the up side of the track, approximately where the first goods shed had been located. This 43-lever box was closed in March 1980 but at the time of writing remains extant and is used for permanent way purposes. In later years the sidings to the north of the station were used for unloading cars from the Motorail trains. There were also some cattle pens at this location but not for the car drivers! The access lines were controlled by a five-lever ground frame. The station had 27 staff in 1927 and a maximum of 40 in the late 1930s. St Austell is one of Cornwall's busiest stations and there has always been an attempt to operate an integrated transport system by having a bus depot located immediately adjacent to the railway station.

On leaving Par the main climbs quite sharply and for the next five miles to St Austell the ruling gradient is not far short of 1 in 60. The main line, seen here in the background, crosses the line from St Blazey to Par Harbour (and in times past, the direct line to Fowey) on arches. Emerging from harbour lines at Par Bridge crossing on 3 October 2007 is No 66129 with four 80-tonne 'Tiger' wagons of china clay. The manually-operated crossing gates are a remarkable anachronism for the 21st century! *Author*

Above: **Heading a 16-wagon freight and a brake van is Mogul No 6301, seen climbing between Par and St Austell with a westbound train on 10 August 1956. These locomotives weighed 62 tons and their tenders a further 40 tons, and despite being 40 years older their tractive effort was comparable to a BR Standard 4MT 4-6-0 in the No 75xxx series.**
Les Elsey

Middle: **In this fine photograph by the late Les Elsey the gradient to the southwest of Par station is obvious, even without the benefit of a telephoto lens. Heading west with a down goods train destined for Drump Lane at Redruth, on 8 August 1956, is No 6941 *Fillongley Hall*. On the left are Chapel sidings, which survive and are still in use, especially by seasonal Railhead Treatment trains.**
Les Elsey

Left: **Rapidly approaching the Crinnis Archway beside Carlyon Bay golf course on 21 March 1994 is red and grey No 47475 *Restive* with the 14.00 Penzance to Redhill vans. The town of St Austell can just be seen in the background, while in the foreground the lady golfers seem unimpressed by the Class 47. Notice the ventilators along the roofline of the vans.**
Author

Right: **From the start of the winter 1993/94 timetable the time-honoured 12.10 Penzance to Glasgow vans was discontinued and replaced by a 14.00 Penzance to Redhill working (where it arrived at 23.35, having run via Bristol). Observed by a couple of local adolescents, No 47503 *Heaton* clings to the curve east of St Austell station with the up working, on 8 October 1993.** *Author*

Middle: **In this remarkable anachronism a 100mph express passenger locomotive is employed on the local St Blazey to St Austell goods! On 22 February 1982 No 50041 *Bulwark* was unusually diagrammed for a local domestic coal train and its 2,750hp would not be required to propel some vacuum-braked wagons into St Austell's 1930 goods yard. General goods traffic had ceased in May 1968 but coal trains continued to run until 1985.** *Author*

Below: **An incongruous sight but an exciting one for the photographer was Class 50 (the class were often referred to by the nickname of 'Hoovers') No 50043 *Eagle* heading four four-wheeled china clay slurry tankers past Carlyon Bay golf course on its way to the loading point at Burngullow, on 22 April 1987. Note the heavily ballasted and cambered track.** *Author*

Above: **Although St Austell station has lost much of its old world charm since the old wooden down station buildings were demolished and replaced by something more functional but less appealing aesthetically, it is still a pleasant place to photograph up trains. With miniature snowploughs in position, No 50018 *Resolution*, in original Network SouthEast livery, arrives at the station on 12 June 1987 with the 12.10 Penzance to Glasgow vans.** *Author*

Middle: **Visits to Cornwall by black-liveried Class 47s were not all that numerous but in August 1994 an immaculate Waterman Railways No 47710 *Lady Godiva* sped by with the 14.00 Penzance to Redhill via Bristol postal. The original down goods yard was on the left of this view but the sidings were lifted to increase the car parking and bus station facilities.** *Author*

Left: **Whenever the weather turned nasty during a photographic expedition to Cornwall, St Austell station often acted as a refuge, especially as a hot coffee could be purchased in the station buffet. Inevitably this was precisely the time that a passing freight would rumble through! On a filthy day in March 1989, one that did not 'get away' was ex-works No 37031, in pristine new 'triple grey' Railfreight livery, making for Parkandillack and Trelavour with air-braked wagons. Note the rain bouncing off the wagons.** *Author*

93

Above: Although the event has been previously featured, in this view, having rescued the overnight sleepers between Lostwithiel and Par and having run round the train, rare Cornish visitor No 56013 in Railfreight Coal sub-Sector livery, double-heads with failed No 47815 as it leaves St Austell for Penzance in February 1990. The Class 56 visit was for one day only and for the record this particular locomotive was built in Romania. It has since been withdrawn from service. *Author*

Below: In this wonderful view of St Austell station in Edwardian times 4-4-0 No 3720 *Inchcape* pauses with an up express while an unidentified 0-6-0 pannier tank shunts the up goods yard. The previously mentioned down yard can be seen top left, with plenty of wagons beside the large goods shed. Beneath the overbridge are some crossing gates, which were replaced in 1931 when the road was closed and a pedestrian footbridge was erected. Note the gas lamps, semaphore signals and the up water tower. *Author's Collection*

Above: **There are three young observers on the 1882 GWR station footbridge at St Austell as a driver training trip featuring one of the new-fangled diesel mechanical units comes through the station on its way from Truro to Plymouth Laira, in about 1962. These units would sound the death knell for local steam-hauled trains in Cornwall.**
Author's Collection

Middle: **It is easy for the railway enthusiast to become a little sentimental when it comes to any item of railway infrastructure which is threatened with demolition. However, there is little doubt that by the early 1990s, after over a century of use, the main down side station building at St Austell was in need of some significant maintenance. However, the decision was made to replace the entire building with a modern structure. The 'Red Star' parcels sign dates the picture.**
Author

Left: **This rare photograph shows GWR outside frame 0-6-0 No 1188 working over a long-disused line at St Austell station that gave direct access from the main line to the up goods yard. Photographed on the 15 December 1921 the road crossing gates can just be seen and behind the locomotive is the 43-lever signalbox, which finally closed in March 1980.** *P. Q. Treloar Collection*

Right: **This June 1952**
photograph shows the sidings
feeding into the original down
goods yard at the west end of
St Austell station. Heading west
is No 4940 *Ludford Hall* with a
Penzance-bound train. At this
time the railways of Britain,
Cornwall included, were still
recovering from the general run
down that had occurred during
the Second World War. *B. A. Butt*

Below: **By 17 May 1976 the**
up side goods yard on the right
was used only by Motorail trains
that brought cars and car owners
into the county from Kensington
Olympia. Such services
continued until about 1984.
Pausing at the station is
'Western' No D1021
Western Sentinel with the 10.55
Penzance to Paddington. More
coaches, including a buffet car,
would be added at Plymouth
North Road. *Author*

Left: Another appalling day at St Austell station prevented the use of the usual fast shutter speeds. At a slow 1/60th second and with a lens aperture of f2.3 No 50001 *Dreadnought* was photographed some distance away to freeze movement, which was fortuitous because it gave a good impression of the crowd waiting for the 15.45 Penzance to Plymouth local of 2 October 1987. *Author*

Middle: Introduced between 1989 and 1992 these comfortable Class 158 DMUs replaced locomotive-hauled local services in Cornwall about 1990, although how the number of passengers that could be accommodated in five Mk 1 coaches could fit into the seating capacity offered by the two-car DMU is a mystery. In October 2007 a silver 'Alphaline'-liveried No 158870 pauses at St Austell, while in the background the signalbox that closed 27 years previously remains standing. *Author*

Below: A final glimpse of St Austell showing yet another wet day but this time featuring one of the big Sulzer-engined Class 46s. No 46042 of Gateshead depot was working the down 'Cornishman' in May 1976. At this time the signalbox was still operational and the down starting signal was at the end of the down platform. The driver is looking back for the guard's 'right away' sign, which in this era would have been a waved green flag. *Author*

8

St Austell to Truro

The line from St Austell to Burngullow was doubled in 1899 and under half a mile from the station was Trenance Junction. For many years the GWR had contemplated a line along the Trenance Valley to serve a number of significant clay dries but although some construction took place in the First World War the Bojea branch, as it was locally called, did not open to Lansalson until 1920. A signalbox was opened at the proposed junction site in 1916 and in the early days there were connections to the branch from both the up and down main lines. Rationalisation saw the junction singled in 1949, when access to and from the branch was from the up main line only. The branch finally succumbed in May 1968 and the junction signalbox closed in the following September. Beyond the junction site is St Austell Viaduct that crosses the Trenance Valley and is occasionally referred to as Trenance Viaduct, which is the same name as a similar structure just outside Newquay station. The original St Austell Viaduct was a Margary Class A structure built on a sweeping curve with eight masonry piers topped by the conventional wooden fan arrangement, except for two spans where there were technical differences to the norm. It was about 720ft long and 115ft high and afforded passengers superb views over the west end of St Austell town. A brand new masonry viaduct replaced the original in 1898. As an aside, the granite cutters and masons were paid just under 3d per hour at that time!

Continuing westward, just beyond the viaduct were Trenance sidings that served a couple of china clay Kilns. The first Trenance signalbox was opened in 1895 but closed in 1899, when the 19-lever Trenance Sidings signalbox was opened. It survived until the sidings were taken out of use in September 1966. The sidings made a complete loop with the up main line. Trains arriving from St Austell on the down main line would reverse across a trailing connection to access the sidings. A number of temporary and short-lived signalboxes were opened and closed during the rebuilding of the viaducts and the upgrading of the single track, mostly in the 1880s and 1890s. In this area this included Trembear and Gover Viaduct signalboxes. The next viaduct encountered was Gover, which spanned the valley of the same name. It too was another Class A, built on a curve and was 690ft long and 95ft high, which was replaced by an entirely new masonry structure in 1898. Contemporary pictures of the era demonstrate how frail looking Brunel's structures looked compared with their replacements

This ancient plate camera study shows the original Margary Class A St Austell Viaduct. Built on a sweeping curve over the Trenance Valley, the structure was 720ft long and 115ft high. It survived from 1859 until 1898, when it was replaced by a new masonry viaduct. Note the typical wooden fan-type upper structure resting, in this case, on eight masonry piers. *Cornish Studies Library*

Small 0-6-0 saddle and pannier tank locomotives were very popular in Cornwall as they were ideally suited to traversing the many minor branch lines and industrial sidings in the county. Many of the early classes of saddle tank were later rebuilt as pannier tanks. Seen here at Trenance, just west of St Austell Viaduct, are Carroncarrow and Trenance clay dries and the 19-lever Trenance Sidings signalbox, which was in operation from 1899 until September 1966. The little tank has over two dozen empty four-wheeled china clay wagons in tow and after pulling forward
it may be setting back into the clay works sidings. *Cornish Studies Library*

but on the other hand the timbers had lasted for 40 years, even though they had to be strengthened and the timbers replaced from time to time.

The main line continues westward via Trewoon until Burngullow is reached. The history of the Cornish main line at this point is quite complicated. A single platform railway station opened on 1 February 1863 at the 288 mile 45 chain point. Opposite the station on the up or north side of the line an industrial complex gradually developed, with most activities relating to the china clay industry. At least four different clay companies were rail served at this location. Also from 1869, when the broad gauge Newquay & Cornwall Junction Railway (N&CJR) opened as far as Drinnick Mill, Burngullow became a junction site. The actual junction was located at the western end of the general area and this is one of the branch lines that remains open, albeit only for china clay traffic. On the approach to Burngullow from the east, on the up side, the first siding encountered is Methrose, where a pair of tracks opened in 1924. Much older was Parkyn & Peters' siding, opened by the Trehidy Minerals Company in 1885. Wheal Louisa siding and Cornish Kaolin sidings completed the quartet. All of these companies were eventually taken over by English China Clays, which absorbed well over 100 independent clay companies in its time. The precise track configuration changed from time to time to reflect operational needs. In later years ECC built some massive clay silos that have become a local landmark, such is their size. In fact the vast silos have been disused for a couple of decades. This entire site became known as Blackpool, the name

of vast clay pit to the north. In 1988 ECC spent over £2 million at this location gearing up for the increased production and distribution of china clay in slurry form, in preparation of a new traffic flow from Burngullow to Irvine in Scotland, where the clay was used in the production of paper. Known as the 'Silver Bullet', the last such train ran in January 2008 as the new French owner Imerys chose to buy some of its clay from Brazil. In previous years china clay had been produced in slurry form for other customers including Bowaters at Sittingbourne and the Crossfield company near Warrington. Other clay products continue to be loaded at Burngullow. An even more recent innovation has been the unloading of stone traffic at Burngullow and the loading of china clay waste at the site, in the shape of fine sand, for conveyance to either Bow or Angerstein Wharf for eventual use in the building industry.

Returning to Burngullow station, in 1901 a new two-platform station was built 11 chains further west than the original site, just beyond the N&CJR junction and a local road bridge. An early broad gauge engine shed adjacent to the junction on the up side was finally closed in 1922 and removed about eight years later. On the down platform was the 31-lever Burngullow signalbox, also dating from 1901. Just before the First World War, during 1913, a total of 9,590 tickets had been sold here but this had fallen to 1,318 by 1931 (nine months only). The station closed completely in September 1931 and in 2008 there is still one small ivy-covered building remaining on the up side to provide evidence that a station existed here. The signalbox was taken out of use in 1986 and after use by permanent way staff it was burnt to the ground in suspicious

This undated photograph shows what appears to be an almost new Churchward '43xx' class 2-6-0 crossing a new-looking Gover Viaduct with a down passenger train, with carriage boards on the coaches, some of which have clerestory roofs. The viaduct replaced an earlier structure in 1898 and locomotives of the class were introduced from 1911. It is probable that the view dates from between 1912 and 1922. *Cornish Studies Library*

circumstances. A much earlier 23-lever signalbox at Burngullow East, also on the down side but opposite the clay works, opened in 1899 but closed in March 1935. The N&CJR line was taken over by the CMR in 1874 and it joined the line with St Dennis Junction on the Newquay branch. The GWR later converted the N&CJR to standard gauge. In the days of steam a couple of trains per day traversed the route but in 1966 the line was again cut back from St Dennis Junction but only as far as Parkandillack. Today the line is still in use and large clay-drying plants at Kernick, Treviscoe and Parkandillack provide sufficient traffic for at least two trains every weekday. In times past there were dozens of small clay dries served along the route but the detail is outside of the scope of this book. More information can be found in the author's *Branches & Byways: Cornwall*, published by OPC in 2002 (ISBN 978 0 86093 566 3). At Burngullow there is a small shunters cabin just beyond the junction and road bridge on the up side.

A rather short-sighted decision was made in 1986 to single a long section of double track from Burngullow to Probus in the interests of economy. However, although the Cornish main line timetable is hardly frenetic, pathing problems were experienced when late-running trains were made even later waiting for the single line to clear. This also applied to trains that were not late but were made late by a similar wait. Nevertheless it is difficult to understand how the cost of full reinstatement could ever be justified. The reconversion to double track was completed in 2004. To the west of the entire Burngullow site there was a long refuge siding on the up side but it was lifted a couple of decades ago. The main line then descends at 1 in 70/84 to Lower Dowgas Farm where the reverse curves have always been specially braced as they pass over old mine workings. The line then passes through Coombe village to the impressive Coombe St Stephen Viaduct. This 738ft long 70ft high viaduct looks more imposing from above, on the inside of its curved structure. The original had piers of doubtful quality and Margary, the engineer, considered in 1880 that the line should be diverted to the north over a replacement viaduct, which is the one in use today. The new viaduct was ready for service in July 1886 and as with other

examples it carried a single-line broad gauge track and from 1892 standard gauge track until the line was doubled in 1898. The old ivy-covered piers dating back to 1859 can still be seen.

Beyond Coombe St Stephen on the up side an old siding serving a tramway that led to an iron mine at Bodinnick was in operation in the 1870s and 1880s but is thought to have closed by 1886. It seems there was a short-lived signalbox at the location. Next up is the Fal Viaduct that not only crosses the River Fal but passes over the lovely oak woods at Trenowth. The original 570ft long 90ft high structure was replaced in 1884 at a cost of £12,000. The line runs onwards towards Grampound Road station, the name 'Road' always indicating that the station was some way from the town or village contained in the name on the running-in board. In this case Grampound was some two miles distant! However, adjacent to Grampound Road there was a Railway Hotel and a Commercial Hotel and a handful of houses, so the station was not completely isolated. The two-platform station was located on a curve and in a cutting with a down and an up side goods yard, located at the Plymouth end of both platforms. The up yard had a loading dock and a goods shed but traffic from both yards was formally withdrawn in June 1964. Most of the traffic handled had been agricultural. Halfway along the up platform was a 27-lever signalbox that was opened in 1898 and closed in June 1972. The station itself was closed at the height of the Beeching era, on 5 October 1964. There was a long refuge and storage siding on the up side west of the station, which was taken out of use in March 1966. The line from Grampound Road to Probus was doubled in April 1898.

Nearly 2½ miles west of Grampound Road was Probus & Ladock Platform, later Halt. The word 'platform' was, in GWR terminology, a staffed halt. However, before the site of the small two-platform stopping place was the 435ft long and 43ft high Probus Viaduct. Trains approached the viaduct from both directions at speed down gradients of about 1 in 100 and it is said that this movement weakened the viaduct. Between 1859 and 1871 the viaduct served its purpose but with concern from the engineers. Accordingly, after a life of only 12 years, it was replaced by an embankment, rather than a stronger viaduct. The halt was opened in 1908 with wooden platforms on both sides of the line and corrugated iron shelters and oil lamps. It was little used and was closed from 2 December 1957 and latterly was unstaffed. Prior to 1897 there was an up loop west of Probus that was also known as Probus Crossing. Beyond that site was the 10-lever Probus signalbox, which closed in August 1965. This was followed by the seven-pier Tregarne Viaduct, the original being 606ft long and 83ft high. This viaduct was in good condition and was not replaced until 1901, when a single line was diverted across the new structure, prior to doubling in March 1902.

Tregagle Viaduct was another single-track edifice, 315ft long and 69ft high. Like Tregarne it too was in good condition, especially following repairs carried out in 1885, and was not replaced by a double-track masonry example until 1902. Just over half a mile west is the 581yd Polperro Tunnel, the line here being doubled in October 1899. A mere 1½ miles further west is the 320yd Buckshead Tunnel that marks the summit of the 1 in 78 climb up from Truro. The line descends through hilly countryside to the outskirts of the City of Truro. Truro Viaduct is the longest in the whole of Cornwall at 1,329ft with a maximum height of 92ft and the original viaduct lasted a commendable 45 years. The 1904 replacement was a masonry viaduct but there was a difference in that the new build was

formed of granite piers but with arches and balustrades of Staffordshire blue bricks. Beyond Truro Viaduct was an unusual facility known as Truro Cattle Pens, where a siding was open on the down side from June 1899 until November 1963. A 19-lever signalbox was in operation at the site from 1904 until 1963. Beyond the cattle pens site is Carvedras Viaduct, the original being 969ft long and 86ft high. The fine viaduct that crossed Victoria Gardens in Truro was replaced by a masonry viaduct in 1902. Five of the old piers remain today as evidence of the CR's remarkable achievements.

The City of Truro is the capital of Cornwall and in 1901 the population was 11,562. By 2008 that population had doubled. Truro has always been a major railway centre but since the mid-1960s the local goods traffic by rail has been in terminal decline and, almost unbelievably, is presently devoid of any income-generating freight. The complex track configurations have changed many dozens of times and here we deal only with the major features and changes. The station has an up and a down main line platform with a bay at the west end for Falmouth branch trains. For many years there was an up island platform, which was later converted to a bay before becoming disused. There was an agricultural goods depot on the down side just east of the station. By 1982 it was out of use and the land has now been redeveloped for housing. On the up side is Truro's

This is the view of the vast Blackpool clay works complex, as seen from Trewoon through a 300mm Nikkor lens. The then twice-weekly train of china clay slurry tanks for the Caledonian Paper Company at Irvine in Scotland is seen leaving the works on a September morning in 2004, headed by No 66115. On the right is the stack of an old clay works while upper left are the vast but now unused china clay storage silos. *Author*

surviving signalbox, Truro East. Opened in 1899 a new 51-lever frame was installed in November 1971, the same year that the 49-lever west box was closed. An engine shed was located north of the station but this was completely removed to a new steam shed site at the west end of the complex in 1899/1900, when many significant changes took place. From that date up to ten sidings were installed and these formed the main Truro goods yard for many decades. A six-ton-capacity crane was available in the yard. Until 1988 there was a through line capability from the goods yard to the up main line. From the 1920s there were multiple sidings at the west end of the station north of the new 1900-built engine shed. There was a turntable in place that was upgraded from 55ft to 65ft in 1924. Also at the west end of Truro station was a Cornwall Farmers siding. It was last used in 1992 for fertiliser deliveries by the UKF firm from Ince & Elton, with a special train working once per week. Truro is unusual in having two passenger overbridges as well as a public pedestrian bridge that replaced a road crossing way back in 1876.

The station was substantially rebuilt in 1898. The fine new station was brick built, rather than utilising Cornish granite. The location was important in that in 1859 it was the end of the broad-gauge Cornwall Railway and in the same year the railhead was shared by the CR's standard-gauge rival, the West Cornwall Railway, thereby giving the possibility of travelling from London and Plymouth to Penzance by rail throughout with only one change of train, at Truro. The railway first arrived in the city in 1852 with the WCR opening its Truro Road station, followed in 1855 by the Newham terminus. The original CR station boasted an all-over roof. The broad-gauge Falmouth branch opened in 1863 and the first broad-gauge goods train ran through to Penzance in 1866 followed by the first passenger train in 1867. From 1876 the GWR assumed a controlling interest in all south Cornwall railway lines. The conversion of the broad gauge was the next major milestone followed by the aforementioned rebuilding. A new service from Truro to Newquay via Chacewater commenced in 1905.

Generally the railway scene was very buoyant and even by the 1950s there were over 100 train workings at Truro on summer Saturdays, including the branch trains. A diesel servicing point opened in November 1959 and the steam shed closed in 1962, followed by the withdrawal of all general goods traffic. In more recent years there have been attempts at running trains of calcified seaweed and even Newquay Steam beer but generally the rail scene has been one of decline. The Newquay line closed in 1963 as did the freight line to Newham in 1971. Many sidings were subsequently lifted, including the lines from the goods yard giving access to the up main line. On the plus side manual signalling survives and lower quadrant semaphores still crash their way into the 'off' position. Also, although at one time under threat, the Falmouth branch was one of the post-Beeching survivors in Cornwall. Even in 2009 the main-line passenger and branch service is reasonable. Staffing levels have considerably reduced since 1903 when there were 66 staff and 1938 when there were 98! In 1912 Truro was the first station in Cornwall to issue platform tickets. Almost opposite the station is the County Records Office and the Royal Institute of Cornwall is in the centre of the city, such status being granted in 1877, three years before the commencement of the building of Truro Cathedral. Passenger facilities are retained, such as booking office, waiting room, station buffet and conveniences.

In the late 1980s English China Clays spent some £2 million updating and modifying the track layout and loading facilities at its vast Burngullow works, partly justified by the new slurry traffic. Having turned off the down main line and crossed the up main line No 66019 passes the works and heads for Parandillack with a long train of CDA wagons from Carne Point, Fowey, on 4 October 2007. The domestic ex-BR Imerys-owned Class 08 shunter can be seen through the heat haze of the exhaust. *Author*

Above: **On 5 April 1979 the start of the new tax year was celebrated by No 50037 *Illustrious* failing at Lower Dowgas between Truro and St Austell while heading the up 'Cornish Riviera'. The author gave a lift to the Class 50's driver from the point of failure (where he just happened to be) as far as Burngullow, where help was summoned in the shape of 138-tonne Class 46 No 46044, which had been working china clay traffic nearby. Over an hour later the ensemble passed Burngullow, the unusual photograph being ample reward in itself for the rescue!** *Author*

Middle: **It was always fascinating to hear St Blazey Supervisor Norman Searle talk about Cornish railways and even in the comparatively modern era he always talked about this daily freight as 'The West Cornwall'. Just after the ill-advised decision had been taken to single the main line between Burngullow and Probus, the 'West Cornwall' produced not only just a single van but was unusually powered by a Gateshead 'Generator' Class 47 No 47407 *Aycliffe*, seen in 'large logo' livery on 24 April 1987.** *Author*

Left: **There is a touch of Scotland in this view of the junction at Burngullow. No 37412 *Loch Lomond* had just been transferred from Glasgow Eastfield to Plymouth Laira when it was despatched to the wilds of Hensbarrow Downs to haul the afternoon air brake on the Drinnick Mill branch from Parkandillack to St Blazey. Note the white West Highland terrier on the bodyside! The disused signalbox was used by permanent way workers until it was torched by local yobs.** *Author*

Above: After surviving as a single track for 17 years it was decided in 2003 to reinstate the second line between Burngullow and Probus. It was thus possible to secure yet another permutation to the collection of Burngullow photographs. Looking glorious in the late-summer sunshine, the Royal Train is seen returning from Truro and travelling 'up' what will soon be the 'down' main line in September 2004! No 67002 is in immaculate condition and the silver buffers are worth noting. *Author*

Below: The 1,250hp Class 25s were regular performers in the County of Cornwall between 1971 and 1981, confined mainly to freight duties. The class replaced the 1,000/1,100hp North British Class 22s, many of which had very short working lives indeed. Using the crossover to gain access to the sidings at Burngullow on 19 May 1976 is No 25207. Note the conveyors leading to the china clay silos and the old building on the right, on the site of the original 1863 to 1901 station. *Author*

Above: **Much beloved 'Western' Class 52 No D1036 *Western Emporer* heads west through Crugwallins with the 08.00 Bristol Temple Meads to Penzance, which in this era always comprised both passenger coaches and vans, giving the impression of an old-fashioned 'mixed' train. The locomotive's number appears in the train indicator panel in this 21 May 1976 view, taken just months before the Crewe-built machine was withdrawn.** *Author*

Below: **Other than for the annual visit by the Chipman's weed-killing train in the 1990s, visits to Cornwall by Class 20 locomotives were an extreme rarity. Nevertheless on 8 June 1986 F&W Railtours organised its 'Chopper Topper' tour and Nos 20054 and 20011 are seen on the down run at Lower Dowgas Farm between Burngullow and Grampound Road. Note the special track bracing bottom left, required to avoid subsidence problems from old mine workings beneath the ground.** *Author*

Above: **Coombe St Stephen Viaduct is set in the most delightful rural countryside, although by 2008 only one locomotive-hauled train per week in each direction (plus the up and down overnight sleeping car train) crosses the 738ft-long structure. Sweeping across the viaduct on the then single track is No 47519 heading the 10.17 Penzance to Manchester on 10 June 1989. Note the ivy-covered piers of the old viaduct at centre left.** *Author*

Below: **By 11 July 1961 steam had been ousted on the crack express trains in Cornwall and the up 'Cornish Riviera' was in the hands of North British 2,200hp diesel-hydraulic 'Warship' No D840** *Resistance,* **seen approaching Grampound Road station, where it was not scheduled to stop. Built in February 1961 and later classified Class 43, the locomotive lasted only eight years, being withdrawn in April 1969.** *R. C. Riley/Transport Treasury*

Above: **The remains of the old up platform at Grampound Road station can just be seen to the left of the 11.05 Paddington to Penzance relief, seen storming through the site on 17 June 1989 behind No 47654 *Finsbury Park*. The station was closed from 5 October 1964 and judging by its distance from the village it purported to serve, the decision was hardly surprising.** *Author*

Middle: **In this 1947 view at Grampound Road both platforms and both up and down station buildings are intact, as are the two goods yards at the distant Plymouth end of the site. A 27-lever signalbox was situated halfway along the up platform between 1898 and 1972.** *Ian Allan Library*

Left: **The next station along the line was Probus & Ladock Platform, later 'Halt'. The word 'platform' was GWR terminology for a staffed halt. The station was opened in 1908 and it boasted wooden platforms, corrugated iron shelters and oil lamps. It was little used and closed from 2 December 1957. This interesting view dates back to 27 May 1922.** *Ian Allan Library*

Right: **Negotiating the perpetual curves of Cornwall's main line just west of Buckshead Tunnel on 24 July 1986 is all-blue No 47624** *Cyclops* **with the 09.20 Liverpool to Penzance. All along the 75-mile route from Saltash to Penzance there are various generations of lineside huts but gradually the majority have fallen into disuse as working practices have changed.**
Author

Below: **On the approach to the City of Truro there are two imposing viaducts, Truro, the longest in Cornwall at 1,329ft, and Carvedras. In this 1860 etching an impression of one of the earliest trains on the line is seen crossing the latter structure, which was replaced in 1902.**
Brunel University

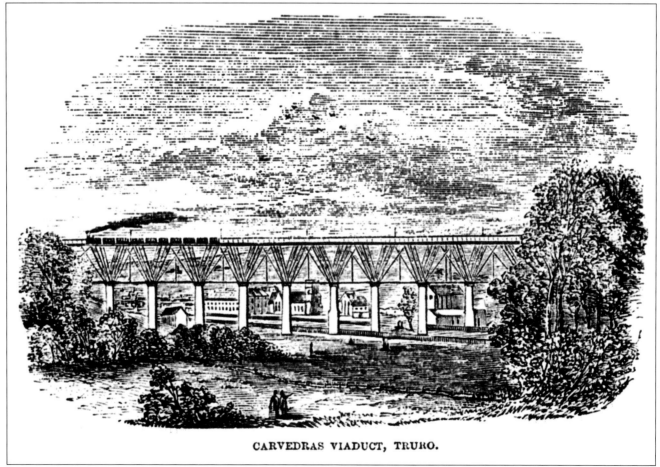

CARVEDRAS VIADUCT, TRURO.

Left: Tregarne Viaduct is beyond the site of Probus & Ladock Halt in the Truro direction. The original Margary Class A viaduct was 606ft long and 83ft high and in this tremendous view a 'Duke' class 4-4-0 is seen crossing the original structure with an up train. The 'Dukes' arrived in Cornwall in 1895 and the original viaduct was replaced in 1901. Note the huge scale of the seven piers, with three men standing on the second pier from the camera being dwarfed by their creation. *Newquay Old Cornwall Society*

Middle: Although hard to believe, the right foreground fence is on the same alignment as shown in the pre-1901 view.
Seen crossing the replacement viaduct is one of the hardest trains to photograph in Cornwall, the as and when required calcified seaweed loads destined for either Carlisle or Selby. The pellets were carried by road from Falmouth to Truro where these HEA 'coal' wagons were loaded. In addition to some 500 tons (gross) of seaweed some rail flats have been added to the train, seen leaving Tregarne Viaduct on 25 September 1995 behind No 37673. *Author*

Below: There was always some lineside excitement when 'required' motive power turned-up unexpectedly. On 9 June 1990 a truly mint No 47484 *Isambard Kingdom Brunel* emerged from Buckshead Tunnel with the up 12.34 Penzance to Paddington, which was quite definitely in the 'required' category. The locomotive would be doing little more than toying with just six InterCity coaches in tow. *Author*

Above: **For a couple of summer seasons this unusual combination appeared in the Royal Duchy at weekends. This '82xxx' Driving Van Trailer and stock would normally be found working behind 25kV electric power between Wolverhampton, Birmingham and London Euston but the formation was spare at weekends. It was therefore utilised for an 07.31 Wolverhampton to Penzance working, which had of course to be diesel-hauled. On 9 June 1990 'large logo' No 47822 headed No 82129 on the descent from Polperro to Buckshead Tunnel.** *Author*

Middle: **The 09.30 Paddington to Penzance was an express in every way and on 17 May 1976 it was perhaps surprising that a tired-looking D1041 *Western Prince* was entrusted with such a train so late in its career. From an enthusiast's point of view the locomotive's appearance was enough to 'make the day', with 'The Prance' seen here at a rather damp Truro.** *Author*

Right: **Yet another railway photographic delicacy is this stunning photograph of not only a train at night at Truro station but featuring a class of locomotive that traditionally has been extremely rare in Cornwall. Standing where *Western Prince* was photographed in 1976 are Nos 31285 and 31233, which had just arrived from Falmouth with a structure gauging train, before working to Penzance for overnight stabling on 10 December 2004.** *Sam Felce*

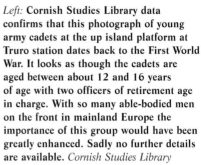

Left: **Cornish Studies Library data confirms that this photograph of young army cadets at the up island platform at Truro station dates back to the First World War. It looks as though the cadets are aged between about 12 and 16 years of age with two officers of retirement age in charge. With so many able-bodied men on the front in mainland Europe the importance of this group would have been greatly enhanced. Sadly no further details are available.** *Cornish Studies Library*

Middle: **The original Carvedras Viaduct was a Margary Class A structure that was 969ft in length and 86ft high. Three of the piers were buttressed and eight were plain, all carrying a wooden fan-shaped upper configuration. The viaduct crossed the famous Victoria Gardens and here St Georges Road is featured, looking south. The viaduct lasted until 1902, a life of 43 years.** *Cornish Studies Library*

Below: **Proving that it was no myth that in pre-Second World War days the GWR kept its main line engines in superb condition, is this photograph of pristine 'Hall' class No 5953 *Dunley Hall* at Truro, on 27 August 1936. The train is the long-distance 10.45am Penzance to Aberdeen. The up island platform at Truro, seen here, is no longer in use.** *Maurice Dart Collection*

Above: **This view shows rather strange operations at Truro on 16 March 1989. On Mondays to Fridays the 12.20 Penzance to Glasgow parcels arrived at the up main platform where it was loaded. The loaded train pulled forward and was then propelled back into the down main platform to allow the 12.50 Penzance to Cardiff to pass. On this day No 47539** *Rochdale Pioneers* **was on the van train, left, while No 50008** *Thunderer* **was entrusted to the passenger train, right.** *Author*

Middle: **A scene that is flattering to Truro, in that it gives the impression that the station is much busier than it really is. On the left No 50039** *Implacable* **arrives in the rain with the 12.00 Penzance to Plymouth while the 07.20 Paddington to Penzance IC125 arrives at the down platform, on 21 August 1986. Note the up lower quadrant starting signal between the trains.** *Author*

Right: **On 21 August 1986 there was a most interesting vehicle incorporated in the 06.50 Swindon to Penzance service train, which had just arrived at the Cornish county town behind No 50048** *Dauntless.* **The WR Track Testing Coach was a modified vintage coach resting on modern coil sprung bogies. The vehicle was crammed with recording equipment but its use on a service train was a surprise.** *Author*

Left: When this photograph was taken on 3 June 1981 the days of handling general goods in Truro yard were rapidly coming to an end. In the past Truro had been a major freight centre and it is hard to believe that there is now no revenue-earning goods traffic conveyed by rail. Over the years everything from calcified seaweed to Newquay Steam beer has been loaded there but with the withdrawal of wagonload freight the yard is now redundant and most sidings have been lifted. No 37142 pauses between shunting duties. *Author*

Middle: The last regular freight haul at Truro was the dedicated weekly United Kingdom Fertiliser train from Ince & Elton. Several wagonloads of fertiliser and similar products were delivered to Cornwall Farmers Limited, which owned a siding adjacent to its distribution centre building on the site of the old locomotive shed. Indulging in a shunting operation before leaving Truro on 24 March 1992 is original Railfreight-liveried No 47350 *Scorpion*. *Author*

Below: Not only is Truro now devoid of freight traffic but the only regular freight train to pass through Truro station is the weekly fuel tanker train from St Blazey (ex-Tavistock Junction) to Ponsandane conveying oil for use by the railways. Although its schedule and even day of working changes regularly, in 2007 it worked down early on Monday mornings. It is seen here passing Truro with the returning empties at 9am on 1 October 2007. With the camera struggling in the gloom at 1/250th second at f2, No 66102 passes the semaphores with seven empty tanks. *Author*

Right: **Even in modern times history is perpetually in the making, although it might not always be immediately apparent. What was newsworthy about this First Great Western IC125, photographed at Truro on 1 October 2007, was that power car No 43042 was one of the very last Valenta-engined examples still working on former WR metals, most sister power cars having been re-engined with German MTU examples.** *Author*

Middle: **Mention must be made of the Falmouth branch service that operates from Truro to Falmouth Docks about a dozen times per day. The branch trains have their own dedicated bay platform and the standard power is either a Class 150/2 or 153 diesel unit. However, on this day a little more comfort was available as No 158870 was working the service and is seen here at Truro in October 2007.** *Author*

Below: **This panorama from about 1958 shows the down end of Truro station to advantage. As 'Small Prairie' No 4574 brings an up local goods into the city, Pannier tank No 3702 has a brief pause from shunting the visibly busy goods yard. Behind the signalbox, which closed in November 1971, is the steam locomotive running shed.** *P. Q. Treloar*

Above: **22 July 1960 was a great day for the steam fans as North British Class 22 No D6312 had failed while working this up express. Rather than taking a chance on the healthy locomotive, No D6316, it was decided to pilot the train with 2-6-2T No 4549, although it is not known where the steam locomotive was attached. On the right, with its driver clearly animated, was 'Manor' class 4-6-0 No 7806 *Cockington Manor* about to take over the entire train?**
R. C. Riley/Transport Treasury

Middle: **Probably the best steam engines Cornwall ever had in terms of all-round versatility and overall performance, were the 'Grange' class 4-6-0s. In this classic study No 6823 *Oakley Grange* poses at Truro with a rake of maroon stock that had just arrived from the Midlands. The locomotive was one of Truro's own, being allocated to 83F.**
R. C. Riley/Transport Treasury

Left: **To complete our comprehensive photographic coverage of the Truro station area this delightful little scene has been included. Beautifully proportioned Mogul No 7333 in very clean condition blasts away from Truro with a milk tanker, a couple of coaches and a van on 18 September 1957. The locomotive was an example of the class that was fitted with side cab windows.** *P. Q. Treloar*

9

Truro to Redruth

In our survey of the main line our journey now follows the ex-West Cornwall Railway main line and we will later return to the Cornwall Railway main line to Falmouth. The current main line climbs away from Truro station towards the 70 yard Highertown Tunnel, beneath the Truro suburb of the same name. Since 1971 the down road has had a reversible working capability for use by both up and down Falmouth branch trains. Beyond the tunnel on the up side is the site of the original WCR Truro Road station, its terminus from 1852 until 1855, when the line to Newham opened. Just beyond that site is Penwithers Junction, where the Falmouth branch diverges to the south west and which is fully described in the last chapter. Viewing the junction from above Highertown Tunnel it becomes clear that the road to Falmouth is initially on a straight section of track with the main line curving to the west, demonstrating quite clearly that the Falmouth line was the Cornwall Railway's main line and that the West Cornwall line was, in that context, the branch! At Penwithers (occasionally spelt Penwethers and sometimes Penweathers!) the WCR line to Newham crossed the CR Falmouth line on the level but in later years the Newham line could only be accessed from a trailing connection with the down Falmouth line. The original signalbox was replaced by a later 36-lever version in 1893 and was closed completely from 7 November 1971, when the Newham branch closed and all movements came under the control of Truro. Beyond the junction on the main line is Penwithers Viaduct, the original being a Class Y structure. The 1852-vintage wooden supports were replaced by masonry piers in 1869 but an entirely new all granite double-track viaduct was ready for service in 1887 and at 68 feet was 14 feet higher than the original but of the same, approximately 372 feet, length.

Just under three miles from the junction on the up side was the small 6-lever Baldhu signalbox, which had a short life, being opened in 1938 and closed in 1957, although records suggest there may have been an earlier box nearby. The lines either side of Baldhu were not doubled until 1913/14. At this point the line is climbing towards Redruth, through undulating agricultural land, for three miles at 1 in 80. At the 305 mile 48 chain point is Chacewater Viaduct. The situation here was the same as Penwithers, a wooden original viaduct 297ft long and 52ft high modified in 1869 with masonry piers and entirely replaced with a granite double-track viaduct in 1888. Just 25 chains further down the line is Blackwater Viaduct, which again has a similar history to Chacewater Viaduct with a new structure being ready for service in 1888. The original was 396ft long and 68ft high. At this point there was a substantial track realignment and in 1914 the Penwithers to Chacewater section was 're-miled', the line ending up two chains shorter than the original.

In the early days Chacewater station had a single platform to serve a single main line. However in 1872 an up platform was added and a loop was provided, controlled from 1888 by a new signalbox located on the down platform. The opening of the branch line to Perranporth and Newquay in 1903/5 caused some pathing problems and from 1912 an up island platform was built with branch trains in each direction using its outer face. The signalbox was replaced by a 35-lever example in 1914 and this was in service until closed completely in June 1977. From 1924 a new and completely independent line for branch train use was laid beside the two main line tracks from Chacewater to the junction at Blackwater, enabling the signalbox at the latter location to be closed. This additional line was in service until February 1963 when the Newquay branch line closed. At the down end of the down platform was a two-road goods yard with a two-ton crane available. The date 5 October 1964 was a bad one for Chacewater when both passenger and goods facilities were withdrawn and the station closed. By 1933 just over 40 passengers per day used the station but this figure subsequently declined. The goods sidings were later used by cement trains from the Plymstock Blue Circle Cement Works that ran via Plymouth Friary until about 1987.

One of the greatest losses to the railways of Cornwall has been the pick-up goods that would stop at every station to set down and pick up a few wagons and perform a little shunting in each goods yard as the need arose. Nowadays most of the land occupied by these yards is used for parking cars, assuming the station itself has survived. On 18 September 1957 'Prairie' tank No 4554 is about to plunge into Highertown Tunnel with a delightful down freight, which would be a modeller's delight. *P. Q. Treloar*

Created in 1903 when a branch line to Perranporth opened, Blackwater Junction was originally a triangular arrangement with east to north and west to north spurs combining with the main line to form a large double-track triangle. However, the little used west to north spur, giving access to the branch from the Penzance direction, was closed as early as 1919. From 1924 when the branch had its own independent line to Chacewater the east to north spur was singled, a situation that continued until closure in 1963. Both Blackwater East and West signalboxes closed in 1924. Although the new A30 dual carriageway cuts through the embankments of the old junction the site can still be readily identified from the road or the

Based on the evidence visible in this photograph there is little doubt that the Truro to Falmouth route was designed to be the CR's 'Cornish' main line. However soon after the line to Falmouth opened in 1863 it became clear that the Penzance route would become the 'main line'. Now merely a branch, the Falmouth line can be seen on the left. Curving off the Penzance route at Penwithers Junction on 12 June 1978 is an up perishables train headed by No 50041 *Bulwark*. Author

existing main line. Just beyond the junction on the down side is the famous Hallenbeagle Mine and engine house, which often features in railway photographs. At this location was Wheal

117

Even though firmly in the diesel era there is something old-fashioned about this 30-year-old scene at Temperrow, between Truro and Chacewater. Running downhill with coal empties from Ponsandane, near Penzance, to Tavistock Junction is Sulzer engined Class 25 Bo-Bo No 25225 on 12 June 1980. The second man and the brake van add further interest to the scene. *Author*

Busy siding that for many decades was effectively used as a goods yard to Scorrier station. A siding is shown at this location from the early days of the line but from 1902 the siding formed a down goods loop with the main line, from which time a 30-lever signalbox was opened. The main line was doubled here in the same year. The siding was closed from 18 February 1963 and the signalbox suffered a similar fate from 10 May 1964. The scruffy site is now sometimes occupied by 'travellers'.

The next prominent site has great historical significance. Scorrier station was originally named Scorrier Gate but it was changed to just plain Scorrier in March 1856. On 1 June 1859 it

reverted to Scorrier Gate before once again becoming Scorrier on 1 October 1896! Running under the platforms of the station was the old horse-operated Poldice Tramway, the first railway line of any significant length in the whole of Cornwall. The first sod was cut in 1809 and it lasted until the great mining crash of 1865/6. A commemorative plaque is affixed to the wall of the short tunnel underneath the line, which is now a footpath. This tramway is about to celebrate its bicentennial anniversary. Back in the 1870s, before the opening of Wheal Busy siding, there were some coal drops at the east end of the station. The 25-lever Scorrier signalbox opened in 1902, when the line to Chacewater

Negotiating the curves through agricultural surroundings just east of Chacewater is a most interesting train; the 17.00 Penzance to Glasgow and Edinburgh, which contains four sleeping cars. 'Large logo' No 47459 has just crossed Chacewater Viaduct with this up working in September 1988. Note the 'SW' (sound warning) sign on the down road. *Author*

was doubled, but closed in 1930 when the doubling of the track was extended to Drump Lane at Redruth. This was the last section of the Cornish main line to be doubled. Ticket sales at the station fell from 25,000 per annum in 1913 to 15,000 in 1933, when the station had a complement of just five staff. The station was closed from 5 October 1964. A couple of miles further west was Drump Lane where Redruth's main goods depot was moved to and which opened in June 1912, the limited space in the station area having become totally inadequate for the volume of traffic. At its peak there were six sidings, a five-ton-capacity crane and a commodious goods shed. On the up side of the main line was the 29-lever Drump Lane signalbox, which opened in December 1911 and closed in January 1986, after a working life of 75 years. Having once handled 45,000 tons of goods per annum, by the 1960s the yard was in decline and it closed completely in 1979 as goods traffic in west Cornwall became infinitesimal. One of the last freight movements in the area was during the 1980s when the Chacewater cement train ran empty to Drump Lane in order for the locomotive to run round its train before returning to Devon. On the up side of the line opposite the goods yard was Sunset siding, a single track that served a local meat processing plant between 1926 and 1965.

Although mining activities in the mid-19th century were widespread throughout much of Cornwall, the greatest mining area surrounded Redruth and Camborne. The irony was that by the time the railways arrived there were only a couple of decades left where the transport of ore by rail made a significant impression on the transport scene, before the metalliferous mining industry in Cornwall died. Nevertheless Redruth has always been a centre of population where most passenger trains have called to pick up and set down. The station is approached from Drump Lane via the curved 47yd Redruth Tunnel, which gives the impression of being little more than a lengthy road bridge beneath part of the town. Since the opening of the station

by the WCR in 1852 there has always been an up and a down platform and double track where trains could cross, the line through to Drump Lane finally being doubled in 1911. A splendid 1888 GWR overbridge connects the two platforms. A very early signalbox was located at the up end of the down platform but this was replaced in 1914 by another box with 34 levers at the very end of the down platform. It survived until closed in December 1955. Located behind the down platform was a small goods yard while opposite, on the up side, was another siding and a second goods shed. However, in total the accommodation for wagons and the space for shunting became inadequate, leading to the opening in 1912 of the large Drump Lane yard about half a mile to the east and already described. The station, which had 29 staff in 1929, was replaced by a fine red brick building in the 1930s, at which time over 100,000 tickets were sold per annum. It was damaged in an air raid in 1941 but happily the station and awnings survived. There is an excellent privately-run buffet in the up side buildings. The station signs now read 'Redruth for Helston & Culdrose'. Located just below the station on the north side is the excellent Cornish Studies Library, where some of the information in this book was researched. Just up the road above the station in St Day Road was the terminus of the narrow gauge Redruth & Chasewater Railway that opened in 1826 and closed in 1915, the first railway to arrive in the Cornish town. Some granite 'setts' or sleepers are still visible between two rows of garages.

The strangely named Baldhu signalbox had a short life, being opened in 1938 and closed in 1957. It was located west of Penwithers Junction and contained only six levers. The small building can just be seen in the left background as the up 'Cornish Riviera' rushes down the bank towards Truro behind 'Castle' class No 5058 *Earl of Clancarty* on 6 November 1950.
B. A. Butt

Right: **Chacewater station was one of the casualties of the post-Beeching purge in October 1964, when many local main-line stations closed between Saltash and Penzance. From 1903 it became the junction for Perranporth and from 1905 the junction for Newquay. Although general goods services were also withdrawn in 1964, until the late 1980s a couple of sidings were still in use by cement trains, which ran from Plymstock near Plymouth. With a Presflo cement wagon on the left No 50014 *Warspite* heads the morning Penzance to Leeds through the station site on 23 February 1982.** *Author*

Middle: **Having just come off Blackwater Viaduct, a '45xx' class 2-6-2T arrives at the island platform at Chacewater with a Truro to Newquay train. These services were withdrawn in 1963 and with its junction status removed the station lasted only a further 20 months before it too was closed. The signalbox lasted until June 1977, when train control passed to Truro.** *Hugh Davies*

Below: **Blackwater Viaduct stands a modest 68 feet above the ground and the present structure dates back to 1888. Passing by on a pleasant 3 June 1981 is No 50013 *Agincourt* heading the 10.00 Plymouth to Penzance. The new A30 dual carriageway now carves its way through the background hills, far removed from the original turnpike to Redruth and Camborne, which substantially pre-dates the railway!** *Author*

Left: Scorrier station was originally called Scorrier Gate but it was changed to just plain Scorrier in March 1856. In June 1859 it reverted to Scorrier Gate before changing to Scorrier again in October 1896. Adding history to the area, the old 1809 Poldice Tramway from St Day down to the harbour at Portreath, the first railway in Cornwall (albeit horse powered), was crossed by an archway when the WCR was built. Scorrier was another station closed in October 1964. Note the milk churns on the platform in this period view. *Cornish Studies Library*

Below: After closure of Chacewater signalbox in 1977, the cement train from Plymstock had to continue down to Drump Lane, Redruth, once it had been unloaded, in order for the locomotive to run round its train for the return journey. However, after the closure of Drump Lane signalbox in January 1986 empty cement wagons had to travel all the way to St Erth to execute their run round. From 1912 until closure in 1979 Drump Lane was Redruth's main goods yard. On 10 June 1980 a Class 45/0 passes Presflo cement wagons with a Penzance to Birmingham van train. *Author*

Above: **Racing the cars on the A30 dual carriageway just east of Scorrier in April 1991 are Hunslet-Barclay Class 20/9s Nos 20904 *Janis* and 20901 *Nancy* topping and tailing the Chipmans weed-killing train on its annual visit. The train was based at Horsham in West Sussex. The embankments of the old Blackwater Junction triangle on the abandoned Chacewater to Newquay branch can just be detected above the last coach.** *Author*

Below: **Delicate backlighting picks out new Railfreight-liveried No 37673 as it passes the splendid Hallenbeagle engine house, which continues to grace the skyline just east of the Scorrier station site. The train is the returning weekly Ponsandane to Tavistock Junction empty fuel tanks. Wheal Busy siding was once located adjacent to the mine, before closure in 1963.** *Author*

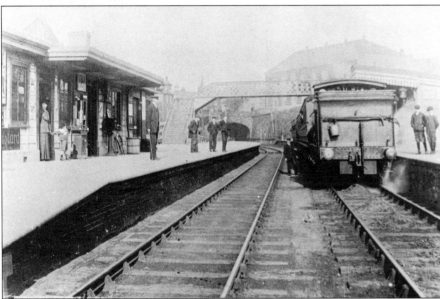

Above: **In this early, *c*1900 view of Redruth station the small down goods yard and the up goods shed can clearly be seen, over a decade before freight activities were transferred to Drump Lane to the east. An immaculate locomotive is seen arriving at the station with a substantial number of passengers waiting to board. The signalbox bottom left was replaced in 1914. Outside the station is a horse-drawn GWR delivery wagon and a handcart. Carn Brea dominates the background.** *Author's Collection*

Middle: **This period piece shows the original 1852 Redruth station building to advantage as both passengers and staff pose for the photographer who was obviously standing in the 'four foot'! The station was replaced by a fine brick example in the 1930s. The train is a down two-coach local, probably in the Edwardian era, headed by an 0-6-0 saddle tank.** *Cornish Studies Library*

Left: **This interesting view shows the feed into Redruth's up side goods yard, immediately to the east of Redruth Viaduct, this being the 1888 masonry replacement version. What appears to be a mixed train has the road on the up main line, although it may be shunting the yard, while a GWR 4-4-0 heads a down train of clerestory roofed coaches in, perhaps, 1902.** *Cornish Studies Library*

Above: **This truly fantastic photograph is the only known example that shows the West Cornwall Railway during its independent years of 1852 to 1865. The scene is full of interest. Below Carn Brea is the original 1852 single-track Class Y wooden viaduct, the restricted down goods yard and the large up goods shed can be clearly seen. The track is of standard gauge (pre-1866), formed of Barlow rails and the original station building looks quite primitive compared with its replacement. Above all the station has telegraph poles, which demonstrates that the view is post-1854.** *Locomotive & General Railway Photographs*

Right: **This busy and cluttered workaday scene from September 1993 requires time to be absorbed fully. Again Carn Brea hill and castle dominate the background. A Rail Express Systems Class 47 is on Redruth Viaduct with one of the last Penzance to Glasgow van train workings, while a Falmouth-bound double-decker stands in front of the excellent station buffet. As a sign of the times the Mining Exchange building at the bottom of the hill is now the Age Concern Day Centre!** *Author*

Above: **Virgin Trains-badged Voyagers in Cornwall are now a thing of the past, the Arriva company having taken over the 'XC' (cross-country) franchise from late 2007. On a very wet day in October 2006 the morning Penzance to Glasgow train prepares to leave Redruth for its distant destination. The windscreen of the air-conditioned driver's cab has two large and powerful wipers, an age away from the working environment of the steam locomotive crews in the 1950s.** *Author*

Left: **Although having rapidly diminished in number over the decades it is refreshing to find infrastructure and artefacts that date back to the railways of yesteryear. St Austell and Redruth stations still have their 1880s passenger footbridges linking the up and down platforms and this example has been superficially renovated with both 'GWR' and '1888' being picked-out by the painters. Seen beneath Redruth's down side awning is up Regional Railways Class 158 unit No 158829.** *Author*

Above: **Redruth is an important centre of population in west Cornwall and most trains stop at the station; indeed, with the speed-restricted curve into the station, a stop need not be hugely time-consuming. Nevertheless a handful of trains have rushed through the town without stopping including the 08.38 Liverpool to Penzance of 18 August 1990, seen here emerging from the 47yd Redruth Tunnel with power visibly being applied to No 47811.** *Author*

Below: **The antics of the photographer are being observed by three ladies on the up platform at Redruth station on 29 February 2008. A typical local train of the age in the shape of one of the austere Class 150/2 units is about to depart for Penzance. No 150239 is in Wessex Trains maroon pictogram livery but it would soon be painted in the current operator's First Great Western colours. The down side facilities for passengers are restricted to a weather shelter but the up side is still well-appointed.** *Author*

10

Redruth to Camborne

The main line curves away from Redruth and almost immediately Redruth Viaduct is encountered. The impressive original curved structure was 489ft long and 61ft high and was a Class Y wooden structure. It gradually attracted a reputation for being in a rather 'shaky condition'. Pieces of timber were regularly renewed and in 1869 masonry replaced timber but only in respect of the braced timbers of the piers. A completely new masonry viaduct was ready for service in 1888, with the GWR looking ahead by making provision for double standard-gauge track, which was duly laid in 1894. A mere 30 chains further west was Redruth Junction where three lines once converged. The first lines were built by the Hayle Railway (HR), the predecessor of the WCR, in 1837/8, with a line curving to the north-east on the up side of the current main line and running to the original Redruth terminus. This station, the first for passengers at Redruth, was just 14 chains from the junction. It was opened for goods traffic on 31 May 1838 and for passengers from 22 May 1843. The station had a single platform beneath an overall roof with a stone goods shed attached thereto (see photographs). There were other sidings at the site that were used for goods traffic and especially coal, until September 1967. However, as soon as the WCR extended its main line further east to Redruth and Truro in 1852 the original Redruth terminus was no longer served by passenger trains. The other line on the down side of Redruth Junction soon formed an incline where wagons ascended to the Tresavean mine area at a gradient of 1 in 15. This line saw use from 1838 until 1935. The original signalbox at the junction was on the up side of the line in the 'V' of the junction between the old terminus route and the 'new' main line. In 1894 it was replaced by a later 17-lever building, which lasted until October 1966. From this time the old line to what was often called 'West Yard' was controlled by a ground frame, which was taken out of use in February 1968. Today there is no evidence visible that a junction ever existed at this location.

To the west of Redruth Junction on the down side was an early and short-lived siding to Carn Brea Quarry from where stone was removed for viaduct rebuilding between 1886 and about 1890. The main line continues through an industrial landscape, all the while in the shadow of Carn Brea hill to the south, topped by Carn Brea Castle and Lord de Dunstanville's monument. One mile west of Redruth Junction was Portreath Junction where the 1837-built HR line branched away to the north to serve the harbour at Portreath. The branch just survived its centenary, formally closing in April 1938; however, it is thought that no traffic had traversed the branch line metals for some years before closure. Just west of the junction on the up side was the WCR's extensive Carn Brea Works, where

It is important to include a little humour in railway photography on occasions and on 12 June 1981 a Penzance-bound IC125 unit was captured on film 'passing' a National Trust sign referring to its fine beam engines that have been preserved between Redruth and Camborne. *Author*

This remarkable impression of an unusual train is clearly on Redruth Viaduct, witness Lord De Dunstanville's Monument on Carn Brea hill behind the train. This engraving by Kershaw & Sons shows what is purported to be a WCR 'Teetotal Gala Excursion' in 1852 but if the three locomotives are broad gauge then the scene could date back to 1867. Whatever the detail the impression is remarkable. *Brunel University*

everything from wagon maintenance to steam locomotive assembly took place. There was a small engine shed on the site as well as substantial works buildings and a traverser, linking a number of sidings containing various items of stock that were either waiting for attention or pending release from the works. After closure of the works, following the GWR takeover, the site became an important goods yard for the area, with several contracted customers using the site, which was also connected to an industrial tramway. On the main line there was a Carn Brea Yard signalbox on the up side of the line that did not close until 1973, the actual yard having closed about 1967. Now just a few gorse bushes and industrial waste grace this once important site.

The original station at Carn Brea was opened by the HR in 1843, when it was called Pool. When the WCR Redruth to Penzance services started in 1852 the station became Carn Brea, only to revert to Pool in January 1854. Finally, from 1 November 1875 the station again became Carn Brea, a situation that continued until it closed from 2 January 1961. Carn Brea was in the heart of a mining area and during 1864 there were 50 mines in the immediate vicinity. The station had an up and a down platform with the main building on the up side. There was a station overbridge and a 23-lever signalbox was located at the up end of the up platform. On the north side of the station was a four-road goods yard that continued in use until May 1967. The station boasted 10 staff in 1922 but in that year only 16,000 tickets were sold, about 40 per day. By 1933 this figure had almost halved. Less than half a mile further west was North Crofty Junction where the short 48-chain North Crofty mineral branch line made a trailing connection with the up main line. The main line at this point and as far as Roskear, near Camborne, was doubled in 1898 and the remains of old mining activity can be seen to this day. There was a signalbox in the 'V' of the junction on the up side, although in fact the building was little more than a cabin containing a small ground frame with a single block instrument and bell. From 1907 authority was given to adapt the ground frame as a block post for the up main line only. The branch was cut back beyond Tuckingmill in 1937 and traffic gradually dwindled, the line closing completely in December 1948 and being lifted in November 1949.

The main line continues to curve its way westward and half a mile beyond the 312-mile marker Dalcoath siding is reached on the up side of the line. Originally a busy coal yard, between 1946 and 1983 the single-track siding, mostly set in concrete, was used for loading milk tankers, several of the six-wheeled 3,000 gallon tankers being loaded every day. Just beyond a nearby road crossing, between the years 1905 and 1908, there

was a Dalcoath Halt, adjacent to the famous Dalcoath Mine, the deepest in Cornwall. At the up end of the down platform there was a 23-lever signalbox, which closed on 21 January 1968 upon the installation of automatic half barriers at the road crossing. At 313 miles and 17 chains was Roskear Junction where on the up side the short 77 chain freight-only Roskear branch line made a trailing connection with the down main line until 1975 and with the up main line thereafter. The sole purpose of the line was to serve the mining industry, whether it was outgoing ore, incoming coal or the transportation of machinery. It is difficult to determine the date of the last rail traffic but the siding was taken out of use in 1983 and permanently abandoned in 1987. Just beyond the junction was Roskear road crossing, where there is a signalbox on the down side. Automatic barriers replaced crossing gates in 1970 but the box continues to control several road crossings in the area. A short siding on the up side beyond the box, known as Harvey's siding and later Saw Mill siding, was in use until 1962.

Camborne station was a HR original. It was located nearby to the Camborne School of Mines and the vast industrial complex of the famous Holman Brothers. It is not generally realised but the population of Camborne has always been greater than that of Redruth. In fact no fewer than 35 staff were employed at the station in the 1930s. The current late-Victorian brick-built station building is on the up side platform that is connected to the down platform by a pedestrian overbridge, in addition to a road crossing at the up end of both platforms. The footbridge is a 1940s replacement for a more attractive predecessor. There are now no station canopies. Despite the close proximity of Roskear Junction signalbox there was another 35-lever box at the up end of Camborne's up platform, until 1970 when automatic barriers were installed and the box was closed. There was once an earlier 27-lever signalbox on the site. On the down side of the station at the western end was Camborne goods yard, where there was a large goods shed and a six-ton capacity crane. There was once a pair of sidings on the north side of the up platform but they were removed in 1937, with the up platform subsequently being extended. The track configuration in the busy goods yard changed several times over the years before the yard closed completely from 5 October 1964. Traffic had been at its peak just before the First World War when more than 76,000 tons of merchandise were handled in a single year. The goods shed survives and is now a retail outlet. The down platform was extended in July 1981. The station is manned on a part-time basis but at least in 2008 refreshment facilities were available.

Above: The stretch of line between Redruth and Camborne passes through an industrial area that was once infested by various metalliferous mining activities, but a century and half later the activity comprises modern light industry. On 3 June 1981 train 3S15, the 12.10 Penzance to Glasgow parcels, passes between the gorse bushes at Barcoose behind No 50032 *Courageous*. *Author*

Below: Over a quarter of a century later Sam Felce was following in the footsteps of the author when he stood in precisely the same spot, as the above, to photograph this unusual train. Re-engined General Motors Class 57s Nos 57603 *Tintagel Castle* and 57602 *Restormel Castle* in First Great Western's black and gold livery double-head train 5C99, the 13-bogie 12.15 Long Rock to Plymouth Laira empty carriage stock (ecs). The previous night's up sleeping car train had failed and both sets needed to work east to avoid a forthcoming overnight engineers track possession. The action was recorded on 5 May 2007, with the comparison of film (above) and digital images providing food for thought. *Sam Felce*

Above: **In its heyday Carn Brea was a very important railway location in that the WCR sited its main works in a location that would become a large up side goods yard. Opened in 1843 by the Hayle Railway the station was called Pool but when the WCR opened its Penzance to Redruth line in 1852 the station became Carn Brea, only to revert to Pool in January 1854, before becoming Carn Brea again in 1875. The station finally closed in January 1961. Surrounded by mining chimneys, the station looked somewhat gaunt on 8 June 1922.** *Author's Collection*

Below: **In the Redruth to Camborne area there is still plenty of evidence of Cornwall's once great mining industry. The remains of engine houses and stacks litter the countryside in a rather eerie way. From time to time there have been attempts at a resurgence in mining but world commodity prices remain volatile. Passing three old mines, as well as the more modern South Crofty installation, is InterCity 'Swallow' liveried No 47808, Driving Van Trailer No 82123 and the 07.31 Wolverhampton to Penzance on 18 August 1990.** *Author*

Above: **A short distance east of Camborne station is Roskear Junction where the branch line to Roskear, which was little more than a 77-chain industrial siding, branched away from the main line, as seen here. Latterly it served the adjacent Holmans engineering works but traffic had petered out by 1983 and the line was taken out of use in 1987. Passing the rusty siding, which was protected by the signal seen here, is No 50030 *Repulse* with the 10.00 Plymouth to Penzance on 30 June 1981.** *Author*

Below: **A rare shot of a cement train west of Redruth, which dates the photograph to between January 1986, when Drump Lane signalbox closed, and early 1987 when the Chacewater cement distribution point closed to rail traffic. No 47085 *Mammoth* is seen passing Dalcoath on 24 July 1986 with empty cement tanks, the locomotive having run round its train at St Erth. Dalcoath mine in the background was said to be the deepest in Cornwall.** *Author*

Above: The siding in the left foreground was originally built to serve Dalcoath and other nearby mines and was known as Treveor sidings. Later it was used for coal deliveries but when they ceased it was taken over by the Milk Marketing Board to load its London-bound milk tankers. The siding formally closed in 1983. Passing the site on 12 June 1981 is No 50009 *Conqueror* with a Liverpool Lime Street to Penzance train. *Author*

Middle: This photograph may not be technically perfect but it catches the atmosphere of the 1950s, as the cigarette-smoking guard notes down the wagon numbers of his milk train in Dalcoath siding before a 'County' class 4-6-0 pulls the rake of six-wheelers forward to join the wagons left on the up main line.
Cornish Studies Library

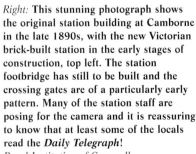

Right: This stunning photograph shows the original station building at Camborne in the late 1890s, with the new Victorian brick-built station in the early stages of construction, top left. The station footbridge has still to be built and the crossing gates are of a particularly early pattern. Many of the station staff are posing for the camera and it is reassuring to know that at least some of the locals read the *Daily Telegraph*!
Royal Institution of Cornwall

Above: There has been a passenger station at Camborne for some 166 years, being opened in 1843 by the Hayle Railway. Surprisingly the population of Camborne has always been greater than that of Redruth and when this photograph was taken in Edwardian times it was 14,726. In this scene a local railmotor is calling at the station and the newish Victorian buildings now seem to be well established. Note the provision of the pedestrian footbridge and the end of platform signalbox. *Author's Collection*

Below: This wider view of Camborne station in the early 1920s gives a different perspective to much of the detail, including the splendid platform lamps, the flat awning of the down platform contrasting with the pitched version on the up side, the later style of crossing gates and the stubby semaphore signals against the covered overbridge, as well as the 35-lever signalbox that survived until 1970. *Cornish Studies Library*

Above: The good news is that the fine brick Camborne station building has been refurbished with re-pointed chimneys (much appreciated by the seagulls!) and a new roof. The bad news is that all station awnings have been demolished, leaving passengers to huddle in a glass shelter whenever the station is unmanned. Worse still, only a glass and alloy bus stop-type structure appears on the down platform and the old goods shed is now used as a retail outlet (left background). In October 2007 it was satisfying to photograph one of the last Valenta-engined IC125 power cars, No 43143, painted in 'old' First livery as it departed for London Paddington. *Author*

Below: A great find during the research for this book was this photograph that would be very much at home in an equestrian magazine! This wonderful scene on the north side of Camborne station was recorded in 1900, the new station having been completed. No fewer than seven carriages of immense variety await the arrival of what is obviously an important train. Note the decorative approach to the footbridge. *Cornish Studies Library*

11

Camborne to St Erth

The main line descends quite sharply from Camborne station at 1 in 61/67/55 and in just over a mile, and having left the built-up area behind, Penponds Viaduct is reached. The wooden WCR viaducts were built to support standard gauge trains and by the 1880s they were feeling their age, having been pounded by heavier broad gauge trains for a couple of decades. Penponds at a length of over 800ft and a height of only 45ft was a wooden Class Z structure that was strengthened and slightly modified during 1861 and in following years. At this time the embankment was extended, reducing its length to 693ft. It was finally replaced in 1900 by a new double-track masonry and brick viaduct, which was shorter than the original. To the south of the viaduct is the site of the original HR incline that was abandoned in 1852. Further west there was a signalbox in operation for a decade or so in late Victorian times at Sandy Lane crossing.

The next location of note is the site of Gwinear Road station, where between 1887 and 1963 passengers would change for the Helston branch; from 1903 the GW operated a connecting bus service from Helston to the Lizard. On the down side of the line, east of the station site, was a goods yard, which in the early days included a transfer shed, necessary because the branch line was standard gauge and the main line broad gauge. Over the years the number of tracks in the goods yard increased hugely, especially after 1944 when sidings were provided for military use. From 1900 there was a 15-lever signalbox at the up end of the sidings, known as Gwinear Road East Box. This box was briefly closed before being reopened in 1925. At the west end of the yard the sidings funnelled into what was, effectively, the Helston branch tracks before running through the station. The yard was used for marshalling trains and in later years for storage. Between the goods yard and the station there was a wide road level crossing, which in fact was the road to Gwinear village via Carnhell Green. Initially there was a short single platform on the down side but the station was enlarged in 1887, when the Helston branch opened and an up platform and a down island platform, providing three platform faces, were built. Further changes took place upon the doubling

of the main line from Camborne in 1900 and to Angarrack in 1915. A West signalbox was located at the up end of the up platform but it closed in 1915 and a new box was opened opposite on the up end of the down platform, beside the road crossing. A pedestrian overbridge was provided, linking the platforms. The Helston branch services used the outer face of the down island platform. Gwinear Road had been a quiet station in its own right with only about 14,000 tickets per annum being issued in the 1930s, when there was a staff of about 15 employed. The great decline started in the 1960s when the Helston branch was closed to passengers in 1963, followed by goods services and complete station closure in October 1964. The East signalbox closed in June 1965 and the West box followed in October of the same year, following the installation of automatic barriers on the road crossing.

From Gwinear Road the line passed some up side sidings before descending for some 4½ miles, to Hayle. At the 316 mile 60 chain mark the course of the former HR line diverged but as this line closed in February 1852 little trace remains today. The HR line eventually reached the Angarrack Incline where the line ran down to Hayle. The main line descends to the most spectacular of all West Cornwall viaducts; Angarrack. The impressive viaduct, especially when viewed from the village below, stands some 100ft above the ground and extends to 720ft in length. The original viaduct was longer at 798ft but built wholly of timber on stone footings and was of the Class Y type. Although a WCR structure, the cost of the viaduct demonstrates clearly how Brunel was able to achieve a remarkable saving in cost by his unique designs with CR viaducts. The wooden viaduct cost a modest £4,000 in 1852 compared to £30,000 for a masonry viaduct and £18,000 for an embankment, hugely helping the cash-strapped WCR. In 1862 the viaduct was strengthened and it lasted a further 20 years before being replaced by a masonry example with 11 arches. Work was in progress in the mid-1880s and in 1885 there were 68 stonecutters and 40 masons working on the site. Sadly there were three fatalities in two separate incidents during the construction period. The double-track viaduct initially carried a

This defective photograph has been included only because of its rarity. It shows the original spindly Class Z Penponds Viaduct. A third central leg had needed to be added to the two leg supports in 1861 but nevertheless the fragile-looking structure survived until 1900. It was the last West Cornwall timber viaduct to be replaced. The date of this photograph of the up train headed by a tank engine will not be later than 1895.
Cornish Studies Library

Above: **Gwinear Road station was to increase in importance in 1887 when the standard gauge branch line to Helston opened. From that time passengers would change at the junction not only for Helston but for the Lizard, which from 1903 was served by GWR motorbuses that connected with branch trains. Passing the up side goods yard at Gwinear Road on 19 September 1959 is 'County' class No 1023 *County of Oxford* with the up 'Royal Duchy'.** *P. Q. Treloar*

single track until the line was doubled in 1901. The track was slightly realigned to line-up with the new viaduct. A signalbox to the west of the viaduct was opened during the rebuilding years and again from 1909 until 1915.

A great curio in the history of the Cornish main line was the history of Angarrack stations. One opened in 1843 and was located on the original Hayle Railway but that closed with the line in 1852. From the time of opening of the WCR, also in 1852, a small station on the current main line opened at the 318 mile point. This was located at the top of a hill accessed by a narrow road from the village. It closed in 1853 but other than for assuming low usage or the possibility of trains having difficulty in restarting on a 1 in 74 gradient, the actual reason for closure seems to have been lost in the mists of time. Less than half a mile further west is Guildford Viaduct that was originally 384ft long and 56ft high. Again this was a Class Y structure resting on seven wooden piers that needed strengthening by replacing the timber footings by masonry in 1862. A masonry replacement was ready for service in 1886, provision again being made for double standard-gauge track. Rather a novelty at this location is the use of the width of the arches to determine the width of the carriageways of the main A30 Hayle bypass road, which passes underneath! Between the years 1905 and 1908 there was a small single platform halt on the down side of the line at Copperhouse, at 318 miles and 60 chains from London via Bristol and Millbay.

The next station is Hayle, an area that is rich in industrial archaeology and history. Indeed had Hayle not been so important in terms of shipping and engineering, the original Hayle Railway would not have been constructed. Sadly parts of the town now reflect the plight of local industry and at the harbour there are scenes of considerable dereliction. On the positive side there are some fine old buildings and there is a pleasant walk beside the well-tended gardens north of the inlet called Copperhouse Creek. Local residents have for years been waiting for a harbour

redevelopment scheme to materialise. The same situation applies at the railway station, which is now a featureless and austere location with nothing to commend it. Opened in 1852, the station had up and down platforms. In times past there was a waiting room, booking office and other facilities on the down platform, with merely a waiting shelter on the up side. There was an up goods loop behind the up platform, and a single dead end siding on the down side that ended in a generously sized and now long-demolished goods shed. Until it was closed in 1906 there was a small engine shed on the up side, effectively in the 'V' of the junction with the Hayle Wharves branch, which curved away from the main line between the end of Hayle Viaduct and the up station platform. The branch was steeply graded, initially at 1 in 30, and gave access to the multiple sidings in the harbour area and along the wharves, serving various installations, ranging from a power station to an explosives factory and an oil storage depot. The branch was built when the HR closed in 1852. There were up to three sidings at the station end of the branch for positioning goods wagons. The branch was converted for mixed gauge working, which took place between 1877 and 1892. The branch closed in 1981 after most of the sources of traffic ceased, the last loads being oil tankers serving the oil and fuel storage depot. In early GWR days there was an East signalbox beyond the station on the up side and a West signalbox at the down end of the down platform. These were both replaced in about 1909 when a new 35-lever box with a cantilevered upper storey opened, which controlled all movements. In that year Hayle station employed 18 staff. In its heyday Hayle station was relatively busy and by way of example, in 1938 over 55,000 tickets were issued. Nowadays not all of the main line expresses stop at Hayle but at least it survived the closure blitz of 1964, although in that year all goods facilities at Hayle station (as distinct from the wharves) were withdrawn. The box finally closed in 1982, after the cessation of services on the Hayle Wharves branch. Until the end the Hayle Wharves goods would be propelled from St Erth station, mostly by a Class 25 diesel, something of an anachronism at the time.

Immediately to the west of the station is Hayle Viaduct. Although the viaduct is only 34 feet above the ground there is an elevated view from it of part of the town and over the harbour area, although sadly most of the old Harvey's Foundry buildings have been demolished. It should not have been beyond the wit of man to have preserved the historically important site intact. The original HR station was beneath the viaduct at ground level and yet again this historic building was inexcusably demolished for road widening in 1948. The original viaduct has as many as 36 spans and was 831 feet in length. However historian John Binding has stated that some of the piers at the Penzance end, above the foundry, were masonry because of the potential fire risk. The original Class Z viaduct was replaced on the same alignment using wrought iron girders placed on masonry piers but with timber decking. Many of the piers were simultaneously widened and strengthened. Additional work was necessary to widen the top of the viaduct before provision for double track could be made and the work was executed 'bit by bit' in situ. The rebuilding was completed in 1899. After a short cutting the line skirts the Hayle estuary and fine views can be had across the saltings towards Lelant and the St Ives branch line. Just before St Erth is the short 93ft long St Erth Viaduct that crosses the River Hayle. Originally comprising a wooden span, it was replaced by a steel girder supported on granite piers and abutments in 1883 and later widened.

The line climbs into St Erth via a 1 in 70 gradient. This is another location where even in 2009 lower quadrant semaphore signals still abound. When opened in 1852 the station was called St Ives Road but from 1 June 1877, when the St Ives branch line opened, it became St Erth. In the early WCR days the station comprised a single platform on the up side and after the St Ives branch opened its other face was used by branch trains. There were some sidings and a loading dock on the up side of the line and a 32-lever signalbox was located in the 'V' of the junction, again on the up side. There were significant modifications during 1894 when a passing loop and a down platform were provided, the junction was remodelled and a new signalbox replaced the original. The main line from Hayle was doubled in 1899, the branch platform was extended in 1900 and both main line platforms were also extended in 1904. In addition to branch line use the up sidings have seen many stages of development and decline over the decades. In the early days the sidings on the north side of the station formed a traditional goods yard.

In 1927 further sidings were laid to serve the Porthia China Clay Company and the United Dairies creamery. Between the years 1953 and 1964 camping coaches were stabled in the yard but from May 1967 goods services were withdrawn, except for the loading of milk tankers at the dairy, where huge volumes were despatched to London. Even that payload finished in 1981 and the only freight of note since then (and now ceased) was the loading of scrap metal into wagons in the late 1990s.

Prior to the Second World War about a dozen staff were employed at St Erth and 30,000 tickets were issued per annum, most passengers alighting there to change trains for Carbis Bay and St Ives, or to be conveyed to the GWR's nearby Tregenna Castle Hotel. In 1929 a new 69-lever frame was installed in St Erth signalbox, when the main line from St Erth to Marazion was doubled. Most of the up sidings were removed in 1982 except a single example next to the St Ives branch, where the connection with the main line was singled in 1964. The space created has been mostly used for additional station car parking. On the down side there were a couple of engineers sidings east of the station that were also once used for stock movements and stabling. There is still a small granite building and a wooden shelter on the down platform and a pleasant covered pedestrian overbridge dating from the days of the GWR. Overall St Erth is a pleasant traditional junction station with a dressed granite building that retains most of its original features. The branch line to St Ives survives and except for the occasional through train to or from Penzance branch trains use the dead end bay. The station is festooned with flowers during the summer months and refreshments are available!

One of the busiest running-in boards in the UK must have been the number of words incorporated in this down side example at Gwinear Road. This small '45xx' class Prairie is about to be coupled to the coaches forming the Helston branch train, seen on 22 June 1956. *David Lawrence*

Above: **This great panorama shows all of the major features at the east end of Gwinear Road station. Curving into the station with the 11.5am Paddington to Penzance on 18 July 1959 is No 6837 *Forthampton Grange*. Above the last coach is the down side goods yard, above the fourth coach is a narrow overbridge across the Helston branch line, while in the foreground are the very wide crossing gates and a good old Austin Somerset motor car – in black livery of course!** *Peter Gray*

Below: **Few who witnessed the station in its busy heyday would recognise this study of complete desolation at the site of Gwinear Road station. Just 22 years after closure the station buildings, signalboxes, crossing gates, Helston branch, multiple sidings, in fact everything except the remains of the down platform have all been razed. Passing the derelict site, which on 30 August 1986 was slowly returning to nature, is No 47602 *Glorious Devon* with the 15.40 Penzance to Milton Keynes.** *Author*

Above: **A great surprise in September 2006 was when a two-car Class 103 Park Royal DMU owned by the Helston Railway Diesel Group was delivered to a point beside the old down side loading dock at Gwinear Road for restoration. It was a short stay and the unit moved down the branch (by road!) to Trevarno for further work to be undertaken. The main line is on the left.** *Author*

Below: **This photograph shows the Gwinear Road crossing gates and Gwinear Road West Box. The Helston branch starting signal is on the left and the up main line signals are at the up end of the down platform, in accordance with GWR practice where there are 'left hand curves'. The 1960s were unkind, with the Helston branch closing to passengers in 1963 and to freight in 1964, the same year as the station, with this box closing in 1965 when automatic crossing barriers replaced the gates.** *Cornish Studies Library*

Above: **Photographs of all-green 'Warship' class diesel hydraulics in Cornwall in the 1950s are not all that common, not only because half a century has elapsed since they first appeared but because most photographers were concentrating on rapidly disappearing steam locomotives. Some even refused to photograph diesels! Sweeping across Guildford Viaduct above Hayle is Class 42 No D807 *Caradoc* with a rake of maroon coaches forming the 10.5am Penzance to Manchester on 4 July 1959.** *P Q. Treloar*

Right: **Photographs of Class 50s hauling everyday goods trains with brake vans are also in the 'required' category. Having been named but not refurbished, all-blue No 50046 *Ajax* leaves Angarrack Viaduct and descends towards Hayle on heavily cambered track on 12 June 1981, with a half oil and half coal train, destined for Long Rock, near Penzance.** *Author*

Above: **Due to a general shortage of film, as well as security implications, photographs taken during the Second World War are scarce. In exactly the same spot as Class 50 *Ajax* is 'Hall' class No 4953 *Pitchford Hall* in May 1940 with a down train. Angarrack Viaduct can just be seen, top left. The cutting here is wide as it reflects the original alignment (left) of the original WCR.** *B. A. Butt*

Below: **Truly remarkable is the only description that could be given to this photographic gem. Illustrated is the labour-intensive activity of viaduct replacement as no fewer than 50 men and boys pose for this incredible record. Photographed during the replacement of the original wooden WCR Class Y Guildford Viaduct, the picture can be precisely dated to summer 1885! Many of the workmen are holding the tools of their trade, in the centre a large piece of dressed stone is about to be positioned and at the top of the picture is a broad-gauge goods wagon. Granite cutters and masons were then paid 3d (1¼ new pence) per hour.** *Royal Institution of Cornwall*

Right: In today's world there would be almost an uprising if planning permission was sought to put a 100ft-high viaduct right across the valley above your village! However it is only from ground level that an impression of the vast scale of Angarrack Viaduct can be obtained. The masonry viaduct seen here was completed in 1885 and this charming village scene dates back to January 1906.
Author's Collection

Above: The author stumbled across this vantage point in an old weed-covered cemetery while travelling via back roads between Gwinear and Angarrack. In this long shot a 200mm Nikkor lens helps pick out large-logo No 47436 crossing Angarrack Viaduct on 3 September 1988, at a time when InterCity branding had been introduced but only half the coaches reflected the change in terms of their livery. The sand hills at Upton Towans provide the backdrop and the sea at St Ives Bay is just visible. *Author*

Right: Air-conditioned luxury on a Cornish local train is featured here. With just 96 seats available for the general public in the leading coach and the brake coach behind it, InterCity Class 47/4 No 47850 is given a vigorous burst of throttle as it leaves Hayle station with the 13.30 Penzance to Plymouth, on 24 September 1993. Compared with earlier times Hayle presents a bleak and Spartan scene. *Author*

Above: In former years Hayle was blessed with a down station building with awning, a footbridge enabling passengers to safely cross the line, a fine signalbox and a modest station building on the up side, far removed from a single miserable hut provided today. With 'Special' shown on the destination blind this brand-new DMU was conducting timetable trials on 4 July 1960, before being introduced on the Cornish main line. The general public loved the front seats where they could get a 'driver's eye view' of the line ahead. *J. C. Beckett*

Below: Although this view has previously been published, photographs of North British Type 2s, later Class 22s, on local trains in west Cornwall are not common. Photographed on 19 June 1962 from the long removed footbridge, No D6315 had by then received the mandatory small yellow warning panel on its cab ends. The down stopping train is passing the 35-lever 1909 signalbox, which was closed and later demolished after the Hayle Wharves branch closed in 1982. The old locomotive shed and elevated water tower can be seen behind the signalbox.
R. C. Riley/Transport Treasury

Above: **Although not all Penzance to Paddington express trains stop at Hayle, when they do a good crowd of passengers sometimes turns out. Crossing the antiquated Hayle Viaduct and entering the station on 30 August 1986 is a London-bound IC125, No 253051, the number appearing just below the windscreen. If it had been raining, the tiny shelter would have proved woefully inadequate for the 22 passengers!** *Author*

Middle: **This 1912 view of Hayle station, looking up towards Camborne, shows the original WCR station building and commodious goods shed on the down side. It also shows the up freight loop on the left. The footbridge is not covered but at least, unlike today, such a facility was provided.** *Author's Collection*

Right: **This most unusual view of Hayle station was taken from the home signal located at the end of Hayle Viaduct. On 26 July 1975 'Western' 2,700hp C-C No D1005 *Western Venturer* passes Hayle without stopping, with an express from the Eastern Region, probably Leeds or Newcastle. Note the Hayle Wharves branch on the left, which descends at 1 in 30 to the quaysides.** *Brian Morrison*

Above: The bunting was out in Hayle on 30 August 1986, but not for the photographer! Crossing Hayle Viaduct with the 07.15 Milton Keynes to Penzance is all-blue No 47602 *Glorious Devon*. Immediately below the locomotive at street level was the original HR terminus but this historic building was demolished as part of a road-widening scheme in 1948. An advertisement for 'Hayle Rugby Club Donkey Derby' adds some local character to the scene! *Author*

Below: It must have been a wonderful experience to travel from London to the depths of Cornwall overnight in a luxurious First Class sleeping car fitted with six-wheeled bogies, such as that seen here. On 4 July 1960 'Castle' class No 5003 *Lulworth Castle* heads west from Hayle with the magnificent W9067W and the 11.50pm Paddington to Penzance sleepers right behind it. Did the driver of the black Standard 8 ever pass his or her driving test? *J. C. Beckett*

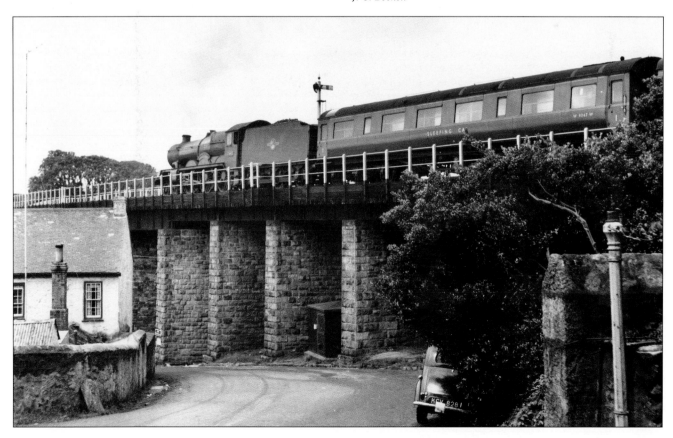

Above: **With a 19.20 departure from Penzance, it was possible to photograph the up 'TPO' (Travelling Post Office) only during the summer months. It is hard to believe that this time-honoured institution is no more. A Rail Express Systems-liveried Class 47 catches the last rays of the sun on a June evening in 1997 and is seen crossing Hayle Viaduct, which was rebuilt in situ during 1899.** *Author*

Below: **This unusual view of the line east of St Erth, made possible only by the construction of the new Hayle bypass (presently a 'no stopping' area), features the short 93ft long and rarely photographed St Erth Viaduct, which crosses the River Hayle. Accelerating the 14.00 Penzance to Old Oak Common vans eastward from St Erth (station visible in the distance above the locomotive) is No 50046 *Ajax* on 30 August 1986.** *Author*

Above: **In past decades the Newquay, Falmouth, Perranporth and St Ives branch lines all enjoyed a handful of through train workings during the summer holiday season and especially on Saturdays. Now only the Newquay branch enjoys such privileges. However things were different in 1958 when the 10.30am from Paddington was booked through to St Ives, with a change of engine at St Erth. Leaving the main line at St Erth are bunker-to-bunker Prairie tanks Nos 4540 and 4566.** *P. Q. Treloar*

Below: **This print features the east end of St Erth station in September 1988. Sweeping into the station at 'quite a lick' is large logo No 47552 with the InterCity 06.38 Milton Keynes to Penzance. The old refuge sidings on the right are rarely used but still in situ, while on the left of the down home signal and the train is the 1894 signalbox, which had a new 69-lever frame installed in 1929.** *Author*

Above: **Although actual timings can fluctuate wildly, the most interesting train to photograph in the St Erth area during 2007/8 was west Cornwall's only freight train, the weekly Tavistock Junction to Ponsandane fuel tankers, presently contracted to EWS. At just after 9am on 10 September 2007 a smart-looking No 66228 enters St Erth on its return journey with empties. It is amazing that the lower-quadrant semaphore signals have survived into the 21st century.** *Author*

Below: **Normally changes and comparisons over the decades are dramatic but St Erth station has not changed greatly over the past half century. No 6911 *Holker Hall* of Penzance shed has been beautifully turned out by the depot staff and is seen proudly heading the up 'Cornishman' in August 1952. The locomotive was diagrammed to work as far as Exeter St Davids, where it would be turned and serviced before returning with a down train.** *B. A. Butt*

Left: **As a down main line train leaves St Erth on the far left, this St Ives branch train will shortly be departing from the bay platform. In 1877 the St Ives branch was the last Cornish branch line to be built to the broad gauge but was included in the conversion process in 1892. In this view '45xx' class No 4566 is the branch engine for the day during the 1950s.**
Cornish Studies Library

Above: **When the station opened it was called St Ives Road but it became St Erth from 1 June 1877, when the St Ives branch opened. In this July 1999 shot, the station, its awning and even the chimneys look virtually unchanged from the 1950s. No 150236 in Regional Railways colours is about to depart for St Ives.** *Author*

Left: **The up sidings at St Erth station have performed many functions over the years. The site was once a traditional goods yard and it was subsequently used for loading china clay. In later years the yard was best known as a milk loading point. General goods traffic was withdrawn from May 1967 and the milk traffic fizzled out in about 1981. Since then only outgoing wagons of scrap metal, as seen here in July 1999, have been revenue earning.** *Author*

12

St Erth to Marazion

On leaving St Erth the line curves to the south west towards Marazion. At this point few visitors realise that there is only five miles between the north Cornish coast and the south coast. It should be mentioned that at the down end of the up platform there was a refuge siding between 1936 and 1988, which dropped away below the level of the main line. Leaving the lower quadrant semaphore signals behind, there is a stiff 1 in 67 gradient away from St Erth station before the line gradually drops down to little more than sea level at Marazion. In early Spring fields of daffodils and narcissi can be seen in full bloom. As trains approach the coast a fine view of St Michael's Mount in Mounts Bay, opposite the town of Marazion, is seen from the down side. Under a nearby road bridge the site of Marazion station is passed. The station was appropriately known as Marazion Road prior to 1896, when it became simply Marazion. At the St Erth end of the station there were some lengthy sidings, used amongst other things, for stock stabling.

In the early days of the WCR Marazion Road had a single platform on the down side of the line. Loading sidings on the up side of the line adjacent to the station were being expanded by 1881 as the growing demand for seasonal agricultural produce required additional rail capacity. Upon doubling of the main line westward to Ponsandane in 1893 there was extensive rebuilding. Another platform was added and a signalbox appeared halfway along the down platform. There was a covered footbridge similar to that of St Erth. The main granite station building was on the

The warm lighting of a late summer afternoon reflects off 'Modified Hall' No 7925 *Westol Hall* as it passes St Erth's home signal with the evening Penzance to Paddington TPO, on 31 May 1952. The siding in the foreground was regularly used by the Hayle Wharves goods before it made its way along the up main line to Hayle. The land is now completely overgrown and covered by mature trees. *B. A. Butt*

This view from 15 March 1951 features a famous locomotive, at least in historical terms. In the late 1920s GWR Locomotive Superintendent and Chief Mechanical Engineer Charles Collett produced a mixed traffic 4-6-0 by rebuilding a 'Saint' Class 4-6-0, including substituting 6ft 8½in driving wheels with 6ft diameter examples and producing a cab with side windows. The result was immensely successful and as a result the 'Hall' class was born. The chosen 'Saint' was No 2925 *Saint Martin* and it duly became No 4900, seen here leaving St Erth with a mixed train. *B. A. Butt*

down side and there was a waiting shelter on the up side built in similar materials. As already mentioned the line to St Erth was doubled in 1929. Two further sidings to the seaward side of the down platform were added to the rail network in Edwardian times and before the Second World War Marazion was at its operational zenith in freight terms. However passenger tickets were in decline with 30,000 tickets sold in 1903 and only 10,000 in 1933, the latter year being at the tail end of the great depression.

Marazion was to become famous for its traffic in seasonal farm produce. Sugar beet, broccoli, potatoes and flowers were all loaded in huge volumes, resulting in scores of special trains. Before the First World World War an 800ft long and 40ft wide goods platform was constructed and additional sidings were provided in the up side yard, which served the local farming community and took some pressure off of the Penzance loading point. It is now hard to imagine the scale of operations. Taking just broccoli, more than 35,000 tons of the vegetable were transported by rail in 1937 in over 70 special trains! Much of the crop was conveyed in cattle wagons, such was the demand for additional freight vehicles. About a dozen staff were employed at Marazion and unsurprisingly the majority were

used in porterage activities. Fortunately the seasonal produce was naturally staggered. There was also incoming goods traffic but this was infinitesimal by comparison, for example 2,000 tons of coal per annum.

With all of this activity it seems strange, on reflection, that it should all have come to an end so abruptly. However road transport was in the ascendency, freight activities were being centralised, spare rolling stock of every description was becoming a rarity and wagonload freight was rapidly becoming out of fashion as a profitable sector for the railways. The down sidings were removed at the end of 1962. If that wasn't bad enough the station was posted for closure during the 1964 purge and from 5 October that year passenger services were withdrawn. The once busy up sidings started to be used less often, and in smaller volumes, leading to complete closure of all freight facilities in September 1966, when the signalbox also closed. Camping coaches had first appeared in the down sidings at Marazion about 1937 with, at times, up to half a dozen vehicles in seasonal use. Various types of redundant rolling stock were converted for use but from 1963 six former Southern Region Pullman cars were positioned next to the sea. From the following year BR decided that camping coaches would become a thing of the past and the facility was discontinued, however in the case of Marazion the vehicles continued to be used by the BR(WR) Staff Association. The siding they were berthed upon was disconnected from the railway system in 1966. Sadly the ravages of the weather, especially the salty seaside atmosphere and the activities of local vandals and thieves, saw the condition of the vintage vehicles deteriorate, one coach being torched by arsonists. They were sold and resold and a few have happily survived elsewhere.

Above: **Invading the land of the copper-capped chimneys on 19 April 1952 was Standard 'Britannia' Pacific 4-6-2 No 70021** *Morning Star*, **which is seen making a sure-footed departure from St Erth with the down 'Cornish Riviera'. It is interesting that the headboard on the famous trains later had the word 'Express' added thereto.** *B. A. Butt*

Below: **So far in this history of the Cornish main line the GWR 2-8-0 and 2-8-2 tank locomotives have not been illustrated. The '42xx' and '72xx' classes also worked between Fowey, St Blazey and St Dennis Junction on the Newquay branch as well as freight trains on the main line. However, in this exceptionally unusual photograph, No 7220 is powering a long rake of empty stock through Marazion station in July 1950.** *B. A. Butt*

Above: All that remained of Marazion station on 30 August 1986 was part of the down side station buildings as No 47421 *The Brontes of Haworth* passed the site with the 12.10 Penzance to Manchester Piccadilly. In the down sidings are a number of ex-Southern Region Pullman cars that from 1963 were briefly used as holiday coaches and then by the BR Staff Association but gradually weather and vandals took their toll. On the right the acres of derelict land were once covered by sidings that together comprised a very busy goods yard. *Author*

Below: One really had to feel sorry for these excursionists who in October 1988 were no doubt looking forward to riding behind a pair of Class 33 'Cromptons' all the way to Penzance. It rained from dawn to dusk and it was wet work even photographing the special. A pair of Class 33/2 'Slim Jims' Nos 33207 and 33211 were diagrammed, which are seen approaching a very wet Marazion with the 'Cornish Crompton Farewell'. There were once sidings on both sides of the line at this point. *Author*

Right: **This photograph dates back to 25 August 1947 and shows an oil-fired 'Castle' class No 5079** *Lysander* **storming through Marazion with the up 'Cornish Riviera Express'. The dark exhaust is something of a give-away as is the cover over the tender, which was effectively a large oil tank! These were the last days of the GWR, note 'GW' and crest on the tender.** *Rev A. C. Cawston*

Middle: **Nearing its long journey's end in July 1951 is No 4087** *Cardigan Castle* **passing Marazion station and signalbox with the down 'Cornish Riviera' express. There was a remarkable amount of outgoing seasonal goods traffic from the up goods yard on the left and, for example, in 1937 35,000 tons of broccoli was despatched in 70 special trains.** *Maurice Dart Collection*

Below: **During 1958 No 1007** *County of Brecknock* **was allocated to Truro shed and on 2 August it is seen heading the 4pm Truro to Penzance away from St Erth. It is hard to believe but in this part of Cornwall the distance between the north and south Cornwall coastlines is only five miles and it seems strange to be looking out over St Ives Bay on leaving Hayle station only to be viewing Mounts Bay on the other side of the train a few minutes later.** *P. Q. Treloar*

13

Marazion to Penzance

With the GWR having taken the trouble to double the main line westwards from Marazion, BR took the trouble to single the line in 1974! Just half a mile beyond Marazion is Long Rock, which was famous as the the main steam locomotive depot in the Penzance area. By 1914 the original shed at Penzance was inadequate and a brand new four-road engine shed was opened at Long Rock. In addition to the shed there was a locomotive turntable, which could accommodate the largest locomotives on the route, watering and coaling facilities and a maintenance capability. There were ample sidings around the depot, all on the up side of the line. A signalbox was opened in 1912 (opposite the depot but on the down side of the line) which eventually contained 64 levers. It lasted until June 1974 when the main line was singled. From 1958 Long Rock depot also received and serviced diesel locomotives, a situation that continued after steam traction ended in 1962. With the impending arrival of IC125 High Speed Train units and the consequent reduction in diesel locomotive-hauled trains the old depot was closed in June 1976 and a massive rebuilding programme was instigated. The new build was designed around the HST, which included a 750ft long maintenance shed and half a dozen sidings, all capable of taking a full length set. In addition to workshops and stores, there was a fuel depot on the north side of the site, which is still served by a weekly oil tanker train from Fawley via Tavistock Junction. Overhead lighting gantries illuminate the scene. The new depot was ready for service from October 1977 at a cost of £1.5 million.

Beyond Long Rock is Ponsandane, although the two are virtually indistinguishable. Since 1872 there has been a siding here parallel with the Cornish main line. During a period of 138 years there has been a long succession of changes with sidings being added, removed and altered, all on the up side of the line. A Ponsandane signalbox opened in 1893 when the track was doubled but it was closed in 1912, when there were considerable changes made to the layout of adjacent sidings. A long loading dock and four long sidings were provided from that date and access to these and movements on the main line were controlled by a new 39-lever signalbox. In the 1930s there were many other changes including the construction of further large loading docks, providing longer and additional sidings for goods handling. By 1977 a carriage washing plant was installed, the eastern end of which was only yards away from the IC125 (High Speed Train) depot at Long Rock. Many of the sidings are extant but with the withdrawal of postal trains the surviving sidings are used only by the stock for the overnight sleepers and occasional specials.

In years gone by the final approach to Penzance station was over a long and low viaduct on the shoreline of Mounts Bay. The structure was 1,021ft long and only 12ft high. During storms the viaduct was pounded by crashing waves, which frequently caused serious damage. The first such storm, in December 1852, was just months after the line opened and 60 yards of the viaduct were swept away. Repairs were effected but in 1868 a violent storm with a southeasterly gale resulted in more than half of the structure being destroyed by the mountainous seas. A temporary line was laid slightly inland but it was nearly three years before the wooden viaduct, which was substantially new rather than restored, was

ready for use. The viaduct was strengthened on more than one occasion before 1920 when in view of the introduction of new heavier locomotives and the still vulnerable single track section of main line it was scheduled to be replaced by an embankment. This would be protected by massive sea defences, a granite-faced embankment and a parapet raised to a height of 3ft above rail level. It is thought the granite blocks used in the sea defences came from the piers of the many viaducts that had been replaced in the 1880s and 1890s, especially Angarrack, although other reports suggest Penryn Quarry was the supplier. The double-track embankment was ready for service from July 1921.

On the north side at the end of the old viaduct was the second engine shed that was open between 1876 and 1914. This replaced the original small two-track shed adjacent to Penzance station. In addition to the long two-road shed the depot boasted a coaling stage and a turntable. Over the last century and a half there have been three versions of Penzance signalbox, all located just outside of the station on the up side. The first box lasted until 1912, the second from 1912 until 1938 and the third 75-lever example from 1938 to date. Semaphore signals were finally replaced by colour lights from December 1981.

The original WCR Penzance station was a tiny terminus. It was stated a few years after opening that it failed to reflect the image of a prosperous railway company and an important market town. From 1866 mixed gauge track was in operation, but the catalyst for dramatic change was the takeover by the GWR in 1876. First, the Great Western extended the goods accommodation and provided the second locomotive shed. The new station was much larger than the first and the site was extended westward with much construction work taking place in the town of Penzance. The new station opened in February 1879. There were still only two platforms with a third line between the platform roads for berthing rolling stock. The new granite-dressed structure had a fine 250ft by 80ft overall roof with weather protection in the form of a windscreen at the country end. The booking office was at street level well above the platforms, and connected to them by a wide staircase. All of the usual offices and passenger facilities were provided ranging from waiting and refreshment rooms to stationmaster's and parcels offices.

With the abolition of the broad gauge there was more scope for modifications at Penzance station. The platforms were widened and lengthened and a fourth road was added to the track configuration. It should be mentioned at this stage that to the south west of the station, where the WCR had laid its first goods sidings, improvements were made. However one of the modifications in 1876 was occasioned by a fire that destroyed the first goods shed. The goods shed was rebuilt but in addition the old engine shed was incorporated in the building work and it too became part of the goods depot. Within the shed there was a 140ft long loading platform. One line extended down along Albert Quay, beside the inner harbour (see photograph). The goods depot was extremely busy with significant tonnages handled in what were still cramped conditions, for example in Edwardian times 45,000 tons of freight per annum passed through the installation. Eventually much of the work was transferred to the new yard at Ponsandane.

The year 1937 was a pivotal one in the history of Penzance station. The GWR had at last secured planning permission for change, which included reclaiming land from the sea on a massive scale to generally enlarge the site. The new station would provide two long island platforms that would offer four platform faces, three under the overall roof and one extending along the south side of the station outside of the roofed area. This was normally used by postal trains because road transport had access to the platform. There would be two long loading docks, one 270 feet in length, located in the area of the old goods depot, which would be closed. The new docks would be used mainly for parcels and perishables traffic. Included in the rebuilding plans was a 1,000ft long 12ft wide promenade for public use. The reclaimed land would enable a number of station sidings to be provided. In the 1930s about 60 staff were employed at Penzance station, as well as road delivery drivers and over 75,000 tickets per annum were sold.

In more recent times changes have continued apace. However the scene has been one of rationalisation with all of the old loading docks in the former goods depot area having been removed in 1987. The land has been given over to the lucrative car parking business. All of the mail, parcels and perishables traffic has been lost to road and even the famous Travelling Post Office has been discontinued, with the Royal Mail preferring its own distribution systems that it can directly control, and moving delivery times to later in the day, to get around the inevitable slowing up of mail distribution that the end of the Travelling Post Offices brought.

In 1980 Penzance station was further modernised and all of the stonework was cleaned. Roofing materials were later replaced and a new travel centre was opened, with the old elevated booking hall being closed at the same time. However no roof extractor fans were provided and IC125 units had to stop outside the train shed to avoid passenger asphyxiation upon restart!

A full and detailed review of all rail services has not been attempted in this history for reasons of space, suffice to say that from five trains into and out of Penzance in 1860 this had increased to ten in 1890, 20 in 1990, remaining at 20 in 2008. The fastest times between London Paddington and Penzance have always been of interest. With a change of gauge and train at Truro, in 1860 it was possible to complete the journey in 11 hour 50 minutes, a remarkable achievement compared with earlier alternatives. In 1890 the 'Cornish Riviera' managed the journey in 8 hours 35 minutes via Bristol, while in 1938 the journey was completed by the same named train in 6 hours 25 minutes but via the shorter 'Berks & Hants' route. By 1965 the overall timings were the same as 1938 but with additional stops. In 1997 the IC125 units were firmly established, having worked the route for almost 20 years and journey times had tumbled to a staggering 4 hours 55 minutes. By 2007, under the much criticised First Great Western Train Operating Company, London to Penzance timings had been relaxed to 5 hours 5 minutes, although a single up train

managed to beat the 5 hours barrier by 1 minute. In 1904 the GWR advertised motorbus connections for Lands End, which over a century later are still provided at the adjacent bus depot. Many other rail passengers arrive at Penzance to travel to the Isles of Scilly, which can be accomplished by a helicopter flight from the nearby heliport, by fixed wing aircraft from Lands End Airport or by ferry in the good ship *Scillonian* from Penzance Harbour.

Penzance station retains a certain charm and the typically Cornish granite structure with its fine overall roof has both architectural merit and aesthetic appeal. The station is steeped in history but the disappearance of railway locomotives, except for the overnight sleeping car train, is regrettable from an enthusiast's point of view. Some of the modern units are extremely efficient and their ride and performance are infinitely superior to the trains of yesteryear. However some refurbished units, especially the refurbished First Great Western IC125 sets, have awful seating arrangements, many seats beckon claustrophobia by not lining up with the carriage windows, the seats have ridiculously high backs and train length is inflexible and incapable of providing comfortable and adequate accommodation at peak times. There is now no question of adding a coach or two to reflect the numbers travelling. Long distance journeys, especially without a railcard, are said to be the most expensive in Europe. Freight traffic in West Cornwall has all but disappeared, except for a weekly fuel train for railway use and it is difficult to find any romance in the current corporate scene. There is no stability in operating companies as franchises change hands regularly and the removal of staff at most intermediate stations has resulted in a shortfall in the supply of customer information and has resulted in a loss of the 'personal touch'.

Nevertheless the remarkable variety of scenery and topography between the River Tamar and the 'blocks' at Penzance is fascinating, with every rail mile revealing a new vista. Over the decades there have of course been many changes and those to the railway infrastructure have been detailed within these pages. But other than for the growth of towns and the changes in the china clay and mining districts, especially in respect of ancient buildings and the size and shape of spoil heaps, a train ride through Cornwall on the historic main line, travelling over viaducts and through tunnels and along seemingly endless reverse curves is an unforgettable experience and one to be savoured.

This quartet of photographs shows different views of Penzance depot, 83G, at Long Rock. In the foreground of this handsome line-up on 24 September 1960 is No 6824 *Ashley Grange* and behind it is No 4920 *Dumbleton Hall*, another 'Grange', a 'Hall' and 'Warship' No D833 *Panther*. This was the third Penzance running shed, the earlier examples being in the vicinity of Penzance station. *R. C. Riley/Transport Treasury*

Above: **Unusually viewed from the coaling stage, from left to right are, No 6824 *Ashley Grange*, 1600 class 0-6-0PT No 1650, No 1018 *County of Leicester* and what appears to be a '43XX' class Mogul. A tippler has been filled with ash and as usual all tender engines on shed have already been turned to face east, pending their next journey. The depot had coaling, watering and maintenance facilities.** *R. C. Riley/Transport Treasury*

Middle: **The old steam shed was later shared by diesel locomotives and following the end of steam in 1962 their successors continued to be serviced in the old buildings, before their demolition in 1976/77 to make way for a new modern installation. Here, on 18 May 1976, just weeks before the old building was flattened Class 52 No D1001 *Western Pathfinder* looks almost abandoned within the depths of the dark old building. The 'Western' was withdrawn just five months later and cut up at Swindon in August 1977.** *Author*

Left: **The long turntable at Long Rock was made by Messrs Ransomes & Rapier Ltd of Ipswich. In this interesting scene only two men are turning the 141 tons of 'Britannia' No 70019 *Lightning* on the 26 April 1952.
The locomotive had worked the down 'Cornish Riviera' from Plymouth and it would return on the 7.30pm stopping train to Plymouth. We can only hope that somebody remembered to remove the headboard!** *B. A. Butt*

Right: **In 1912, shortly before the new locomotive depot at Long Rock was opened by the GWR, this 64-lever signalbox was built on the down side of the line, backing onto the shore of Mounts Bay. It lasted until 1974 when the curious decision was taken to single the main line from a point west of Marazion to just east of Penzance station.**
Lens of Sutton

Middle: **Far removed from heading a Class 1 express train is this almost amusing image of a very shiny No 4083 *Abbotsbury Castle* passing Ponsandane on 9 April 1960 with two cattle wagons, and a brake van, bound for nearby Marazion, where the wagons will be incorporated in a much larger train before heading 'up country'. The photographer needed to beware that a train was due on the down line.** *P. Q. Treloar*

Below: **Compared with today's sleek five-car Voyager units this is what could be called a proper train. A massive 13-coach 'Cornish Riviera' gets into its stride behind No 6940 *Didlington Hall* as the locomotive does its best to accelerate, a few hundred yards from Penzance station on 17 April 1954. There can surely be no greater accolade than to be entrusted with this prestigious train and in performance terms it says a great deal for the 'Halls', one of Swindon's greatest products.**
B. K. B. Green

Above: **With the calm seas of Mounts Bay on the right, an unusual duo in the shape of Nos 25155 and 37299 are seen from the signalbox, just outside of Penzance station, while running round the RPPR (Railway Pictorial Publications Railtours) 'Penzance Pullman' during 1980. The special was organised by the author and his late friend John Frith. The train worked from Paddington to 'the blocks' via St Dennis Junction (reverse)! It comprised eight first class opens, four restaurant cars (evenly distributed throughout the train) and a brake coach. The fare was £23 first class return, including three meals. The train was full and it was a memorable day!** *Author*

Below: **This view illustrates the single-track main line at Ponsandane with IC125 No 253018 seen approaching Penzance with a train from Paddington. On the left the TPO stock is in Ponsandane sidings, immediately above the High Speed Train is the new Long Rock locomotive depot and to its right are the floodlights of the IC125 and sleeping car coach stabling point. The view dates back to 30 August 1986.** *Author*

Right: The final approach to Penzance once comprised a 12ft high, 1,012 ft long viaduct, or perhaps more accurately, wooden causeway. Over the years this was regularly damaged by heavy seas. In fact, just after opening in 1852, 60 yards of the structure were simply swept away. This happened time and time again until in 1920, prompted by the introduction of heavier locomotives, the vulnerable section of track was replaced by a wide embankment. In about 1899 'Duke' 4-4-0 No 3273 *Amorel* leaves Penzance across the structure with the up 'Cornishman'. The locomotive was rebuilt as a 'Bulldog' class in February 1902. *Ian Allan Library*

Middle: Although rebuilding and changes in track layout have occurred at Penzance on many occasions, the year 1937 was significant in that the GWR obtained planning permission to reclaim considerable amounts of land from the sea and to widen and extend the total railway infrastructure. In this fascinating view a temporary track has been laid for a mobile crane to convey large rocks from an attached railway wagon to the point of foundation. There seems to be as many officials on hand as workers!
Cornish Studies Library

Below: Although their origins were firmly with the GWR, the chunky 55-ton '94xx' class 0-6-0PTs were introduced by Hawksworth from 1947 and thus many of the class were delivered in the days of British Railways. Several of the class could be found at work in Cornwall, especially during the 1950s.
On 23 September 1959 No 9434 was busy with an empty stock train, described by the photographer as 'the stock from the "Royal Duchy" and the two Penzance to Glasgow coaches', just outside of the terminus. *P. Q. Treloar*

Above: **Here we see a classic GWR 4-4-0 No 3395 *Tasmania* awaiting departure from Penzance in about 1930. Before the arrival of the mixed traffic 4-6-0s and the increasing weight of trains, four-coupled locomotives were the preferred traction for passenger trains in Cornwall. The guard is keeping an eye on the photographer, while a gentleman on the right is admiring the engine. Enamel advertisements for Pears soap, Nestles chocolate, Robertsons marmalade and Players Navy Cut cigarettes appear on the retaining wall, as well as 'Burgoynes Harvest Burgundy'.** *Maurice Dart Collection*

Below: **A nice crisp shot of a down semi-fast train comprised largely of compartment coaches, plus a couple of four-wheeled vans, arriving at the terminus in April 1955 behind No 4936 *Kinlet Hall*. The signalbox can be seen above the second and third coaches and the water tower associated with the second, pre-1914, engine shed is visible on the extreme right. By this time Penzance had four platforms, three of which were partly inside the all-over roof.** *Maurice Dart Collection*

Right: The '83G' headcode disc confirms that on 17 June 1956 No 4908 *Broome Hall* was a Penzance engine. The van train has just arrived at Platform 4, which is outside of the overall roof area. On the right are extensive loading platforms used for everything from parcels to perishables and now completely razed to provide more parking space for the ever-growing number of automobiles. *Hugh Davies*

Above: Although it is easy to be romantic about the age of steam, locomotives needed more servicing, frequent water and coal replenishment and regular turning. They were not immediately available at the touch of a button, produced mountains of ash and offered a poor working environment for train crews. Once teething troubles were sorted out, the diesels were considerably more efficient, with high availability figures, requiring fewer locomotives and in Type 3 and 4 classifications were better performers, especially in terms of acceleration. On 24 September 1960 all-green No D820 *Grenville* will shortly be heading for the Midlands with train 1M99. *R. C. Riley/Transport Treasury*

Right: The unsung 350hp Class 08 diesel-electric shunters have been residents of Penzance for over 40 years. Often employed on local trips and stock working, their work has hugely diminished with the advent of IC125 and Voyager units and the disappearance of various van and parcels trains. Here No 08641 is seen at Ponsandane on 3 June 1981 with some good old Mk 1 coaches. *Author*

Above: **Early evening at Penzance on 9 July 1953 finds the station deserted except for No 5023 *Brecon Castle* on a three-vehicle milk train that will pick up additional tankers on its journey through Cornwall. Immediately behind the milk train is the stock for the up TPO, while no fewer than seven railmen populate the end of Platforms 3 and 4. Note the various postal and perishables vans in the background.** *C. R. L. Coles*

Below: **In June 1997, the author unintentionally stood in Lewis Coles' footprints by the retaining wall overlooking Penzance station. The one amazing similarity is the position of the TPO stock which, give or take a yard, is in precisely the same spot at Platform 4. A large red and grey Class 47 Rail express systems diesel has replaced the BR 'Castle' class steam engine, the semaphore signals have gone, a massive amount of land has been reclaimed from the sea and the postal van sidings have given way to the motor car. The reference point for comparison is the old sea wall and the distant parish church. No 47772 would soon be on its way.** *Author*

Above: **Another photograph from the early part of the 20th century shows the terminus at a time when there were just two platforms under the overall roof. Some well-dressed passengers are boarding the 'Cornish Riviera' at Platform 1, while an 0-6-0 saddle tank indulges in some stock movement. All of the road vehicles are horse drawn.**
Cornish Studies Library

Middle: **This photograph shows why it was thought necessary to rebuild the Penzance station area. As populations and public mobility increased the train service improved in frequency and with the 'external' platform on the left being used for van trains just two platforms proved to be inadequate. In this 1920s view No 5024 Carew Castle leaves Platform 1, while Opies Hotel seems to have a prime position for its advertising hoarding. Note the first engine shed on the left.**
P. Q. Treloar Collection

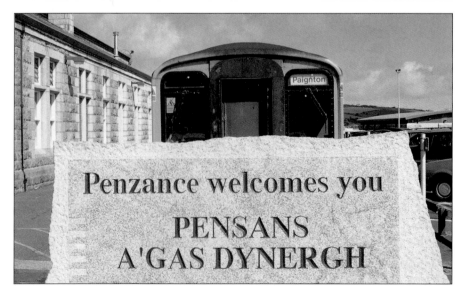

Right: **This is the clear message that now greets rail travellers adjacent to the station entrance. One wonders how many locals or visitors will be reading the Cornish/Celtic bilingual element of the sign. Peeping over the top of the vast block of stone is a Class 150/2 that seems to have taken the wrong line at Aller Junction!** *Author*

164

Above: **Showing the fine overall roof to advantage is this shot of a Regional Railways Class 122 'bubble car' on an extremely wet day in August 1992. The train, which includes a two-car Metro-Cammell unit, is one of a handful that during the day worked through from Penzance to St Ives. The roof was replaced during the 1980s and all of the largely granite stone work was cleaned.** *Author*

Below: **The classic Penzance terminus photograph featuring the famous 'Cornish Riviera' on 9 July 1953, a time when British Railways was recovering from the problems caused by the Second World War. With both driver and fireman posing for the photographer, No 6949 *Haberfield Hall*, with its two express passenger headlamps on the buffer beam, will work as far as Plymouth.** *C. R. L. Coles*

Above: A book on the Cornish main line would not be complete without a picture of the ever popular No D1015 *Western Champion*, which has been beautifully restored and is in great demand for railtours. Having worked in on the 08.00 Bristol Temple Meads to Penzance, the 2,700hp diesel hydraulic is about to return east with the 13.55 departure for Birmingham New Street, on 18 May 1976. A sign above the third coach reads 'Motorail Terminal'. *Author*

Below: The one and only visit of an English Electric 1Co-Co1 Class 40 to the Royal Duchy occurred on 9 November 1985 and it was a long overnight haul from Sussex, via Paddington, to photograph the beast. The green-liveried 136-ton 'Whistler' No D200/40122 was working 'The Penzance Fryer' railtour from Manchester. *Author*

Above: **The GWR was a pioneer in the development of bus services in Cornwall. From 1903 it was running down to the Lizard from Helston and just a year later it was running buses from Marazion and Penzance to Lands End. By 1904 it was running 36 buses and the fleet would later exceed 100 vehicles! This event is believed to be the inaugural service from Marazion to Newlyn on 10 March 1904, with Milnes-Daimler AF 65 full to the gunnels outside Penzance station.** *Maurice Dart Collection*

Below: **Although there were plenty of mine and quarry narrow-gauge railways west of Penzance, the westernmost standard-gauge line in the England connected to the national network is the buffer stops at the station but a near rival was the end of the siding that continued through the original goods yard onto Albert Quay. Abandoned many decades ago, the track survives in places and is seen here in February 2008. The terminus building is quite substantial in the middle distance, behind the tent-shaped roofs.** *Author*

14

Truro to Falmouth and Newham

Returning to the original plans for the Cornwall Railway's main line from Plymouth to Falmouth, these were published in a Bill during 1846 and later passed in an Act of Parliament. As mentioned in the background chapter the composition of the CR was largely made up of a consortium of Associated Companies including the Great Western Railway, the Bristol & Exeter Railway and the South Devon Railway, which provided more than one third of a million pounds in working capital, a fortune in those days. It was entirely logical at the time that Falmouth should be the chosen terminus of the proposed main line. Although in ancient times Penryn was the most important town in the area south of Truro, once King Henry VIII had built Pendennis Castle and St Mawes Castle to protect Carrick Roads and its many inlets from invasion, Falmouth was very much 'on the map'. The town received its Royal Charter in 1661 and in 1688 it became a Packet Station with mails sent to and received from foreign countries worldwide. Consequently the town grew quickly, reaching 10,000 by late Victorian times. Although Falmouth lost its packet status in 1852 the town was growing as a port and the Falmouth Docks Company was formed in 1859. The broad-gauge railway from Truro arrived in the town in 1863 and soon after, what was claimed to be the first tourist hotel in the county was built, providing competition to the common hostelries and coaching inns.

The first sod was cut in a field near Truro in 1847 and construction of the railway line to Falmouth began soon afterwards. However, the railway and its primary contractor soon ran into financial difficulties and work was suspended, with all efforts being concentrated on the Plymouth to Truro section. Even on that part of the main line a cost-cutting programme was introduced, which resulted in the main line being restricted to mostly single track and the proposed branch

lines being axed from the scheme, at least for the time being. In the meantime the West Cornwall Railway had been pressing on with its standard gauge main line up from Penzance and it reached the outskirts of Truro in August 1852, when its Truro Road station at Highertown was opened and services to Penzance commenced. This station was not conveniently located, between what is now known as Penwithers Junction and the western end of Highertown Tunnel. The WCR embarked on a 2½-mile extension that would cross the proposed CR Falmouth line on the level at Penwithers Junction and in a large 90-degree curve terminate at Newham on the banks of the river just south of Truro.

The new terminus was ready for service in April 1855, whereupon the WCR closed its Truro Road station and diverted all traffic to Newham. After leaving the junction at Penwithers the branch proceeded in a curve and in Victorian times, about a mile from the junction, there was a short goods siding on the south side that served the Calenick Smelting Works. At the two mile marker on the north side of the line was a latecomer to the branch, a single siding that divided into two roads with crossovers, which served the local gas works. It was opened in April 1955 but was closed by 1970 when owned by the South Western Gas Board. The branch terminated just 29 chains further along the line, at 2 miles 31 chains from the junction. There was a goods shed at the end of the branch plus the last original WCR station, which had a single short platform and an overall roof, largely of wooden construction. There were adjacent sidings on both sides of the line and one siding specifically served the quay beside the Truro River. A three ton capacity crane was available. Sidings were gradually removed and after the gas works siding closed the line soon succumbed, closing completely in November 1971. Newham's life as a passenger terminus was short-lived, opening in April 1855 and

The Falmouth branch finally opened in 1863 after a series of 'stop/start' episodes. The line was expensive to construct as there were eight major viaducts and two tunnels on the line. In the foreground is the WCR main line to Penzance while in the background is Penwithers Viaduct, a Margary Class A structure with ten piers with timber fans. Work commenced on the viaduct in 1853 but ceased in 1854. It recommenced in 1861 and was completed in time for opening in 1863. *Cornish Studies Library*

closing in September 1863. From May 1859 all traffic was diverted to the CR/WCR main line station at Truro, on the present site, except for the first train in the morning to Penzance and the last train back from Penzance in the evening. The Newham line closed to passengers just three weeks after the Truro to Falmouth line finally opened. During its later years the little freight branch received a daily train, although towards the end of its life this was on an 'as required' basis. The line served a useful purpose for over a century, an achievement that should not be underestimated.

Once the Plymouth to Truro broad-gauge line had been opened in 1859 manpower and finances were diverted to the Falmouth line, where work had been suspended for some time.

Penwithers Viaduct underwent major repairs on several occasions, including a major overhaul in 1887. However it lasted until 1926 when a decision was made to replace it with an embankment. The viaduct was literally buried, except for the timbers at the upper levels. In this 1926 view a small internal combustion engined locomotive has a number of stone-filled tipplers in tow as a gang of eight plus the gaffer pose for the camera.
Maurice Dart Collection

An Act of Parliament in 1861 had formally renewed the powers for the Falmouth extension, which was to be run by a new Joint Committee. Construction recommenced but the line was difficult to build with eight major viaducts, two tunnels and

Continuing the Brunel/Brereton/Margary theme, here we show Perran Viaduct, which was 339ft long and 56ft high. The Class A1 structure had six masonry piers and, following a health check in 1887, it was reported to be in good general condition. It was not replaced by a masonry viaduct until 1927.
Brunel University

In this delightful little cameo the Falmouth branch train comprising a Prairie 2-6-2T, three bogie coaches, an elegant six-wheeler and a little four-wheeled horsebox is crossing Ponsanooth Viaduct in the 1920s. At 139 feet the viaduct was the highest on the branch line. It was a Margary Class B viaduct but with a strengthened balustrade. It was replaced by a new masonry viaduct in 1930. *Cornish Studies Library*

numerous deep cuttings. These structures are described below on our tour of the line. Bearing in mind the difficult terrain, it took just over two years from the building restart for the line to be completed and services commenced on 24 August 1863. At that time there were two intermediate stations; Perran (which became Perranwell on 19 February 1864) and Penryn. In common with the CR main line the viaducts had wooden upper structures located on masonry piers. They cost some £10,000 per annum to maintain and 55 men were employed full time on such maintenance. Hence the savings on capital outlay by the method of construction was gradually eroded by running costs. All were to be replaced or rebuilt during the following 70 years. The GWR formally took over the line in 1889, which was converted to standard gauge in 1892.

On leaving Truro for Falmouth the main line to Penzance is used through Highertown Tunnel to Penwithers Junction where, reflecting the original plans of the CR, the Falmouth line heads south west in a straight line with the double track line to Penzance curving to the right, or due west. At this point the main line was not doubled from Truro until 1893 and westward towards Chacewater in 1914. Prior to 1893 the Penzance and Falmouth lines ran parallel to each other from Truro to Penwithers, in the early days the CR being broad gauge and the WCR standard gauge and later dual gauge. The 36-lever signalbox at Penwithers was on the up side of the branch, in the 'V' of the junction, but it finally closed in November 1971,

when the branch line to Newham also closed. From that date branch diesel trains used the down main line in both directions as far as Truro station.

Following Penwithers Junction was Penwithers Viaduct, which was 813ft long and 90ft high. The Margary Type A structure had been started in 1853 but between 1854 and 1861 all work was suspended, until the engineer Brereton got to grips with the viaduct of 10 masonry piers that had timber fans resting on each of the piers. Over the years the viaduct was repaired many times but by 1926 the original proposal to replace it with an all masonry viaduct was rejected and it was decided that a huge embankment would be built instead. The line then passes through a 924ft-long cutting before entering the 491yd Sparnock Tunnel beyond which the line falls at 1 in 88/64 to the site of Ringwell Viaduct. This 366ft-long and 70ft-high structure had been scheduled for replacement in 1880 but it remained in relatively good condition and continued in everyday service until 1933 when in September it too was replaced by an embankment. About half a mile before Perranwell station and about three miles from Penwithers Junction is the 756ft long and 96ft high Carnon Viaduct, which once crossed not only the river valley but also the tracks of the old 1826 Redruth & Chasewater Railway that until 1915 ran down from the mining district of St Day and Gwennap to the quays at Devoran on Restronguet Creek. Brereton encountered some difficulty in providing sound foundations for the eleven masonry piers and special support arrangements had to be made for the central five piers. In the early 1930s plans were put in hand for a replacement all-masonry viaduct with nine piers, to be located to the south of the original. This was opened for traffic in June 1933, the final bill being £40,000. The remains of many of the old piers can still be seen today.

The line curves off the viaduct and enters Perranwell station. Here the single line entered a passing loop with both up and down platforms, which were both in use until April 1966, when the loop was taken out of service by removal of the former up line and the unusual 1894-built 21-lever elevated signalbox was closed. The loop was extended at both the up and down ends in 1930. On the down side was a small goods yard comprising three sidings and a goods shed, but freight facilities were withdrawn from January 1965. A cattle dock had been added in 1907 and the third siding was not added until 1921. One of the sidings ran beneath the elevated signalbox and a camping coach was part of the scenery between 1936 and 1939 and again between 1952 and 1964. The last freight loaded at Perranwell was wagons of sugar beet. All staff were removed in May 1968 and the fine stone station building abandoned, with now only a small shelter providing any creature comforts for the handful of passengers.

Perran Viaduct followed about a mile from Perranwell station. At 339ft in length and 56ft in height this was a modest affair comprising five piers with the customary wooden fan upper structure. It was replaced by a masonry example on the down side in 1927. Beyond the viaduct is the 374yd Perran Tunnel. The line climbs at 1 in 60 to Ponsanooth Viaduct of the Margary Class B type, which crossed the valley of the River Kennall. At 139 feet this was the highest viaduct on the Falmouth line and the fourth highest in Cornwall, with a length of 645 feet. A report from 1887 suggested that some replacement work was needed to keep Ponsanooth in good shape operationally but in the event the original viaduct lasted until 1930 when a fine new masonry viaduct, capable of taking double track should the need ever have arisen, opened for service. A short distance beyond Ponsanooth was the six-pier Pascoe Viaduct, 390ft long and 70ft high. In 1923 this viaduct was completely bypassed when the track was realigned along a new and substantial embankment, with culverts, to the west of the original location. The line continues through undulating, rural and mainly agricultural countryside.

About 1½ miles towards Falmouth was Penryn Viaduct, 342ft long and 83ft high. Supported on five masonry piers, this was another example where in 1923 a wooden-topped fan viaduct was completely replaced by an embankment on a new alignment to the east of the original. This realignment was part of a much wider scheme that involved the slight repositioning of Penryn station on a straighter alignment than hitherto. In medieval times Penryn had been a far more important town than Falmouth with plenty of maritime activity, including a fishing port. The topography dictated that the station was on high ground towards the back, or west, of the town. Originally the station boasted a passing loop with an up and a down platform. There was a quite substantial goods yard on the down side with a sturdy six-ton crane and goods shed. The goods yard was a focal point for farmers from many miles around and in its heyday large tonnages were shipped from Penryn. The first signalbox was about one third of the way along the down platform. As a result of the 1923 changes the old box was closed and a new 32-lever signalbox was opened at the far end

This close-up of Penryn Viaduct shows to advantage the remarkable use of timber in the structure of a Margary Class A viaduct. The curved alignment with the fan-shaped timbers resting on masonry (often granite) piers was typical of such structures throughout Cornwall. To some extent they were built 'on the cheap' but nevertheless they lasted for between 10 and 71 years. The viaduct was replaced by an embankment in 1923, seen behind the viaduct in this official 1924 photograph. *GWR/Ian Allan Library*

of the new down platform, adjacent to the goods yard. The two platforms were extended at the same time at the up ends. There were also two sidings laid behind the down platform, at the up end. Between 1934 and 1938 there were camping coaches located in the goods yard. The doom and gloom descended upon Penryn station in November 1971 when the passing loop was abandoned and the up road later removed. The goods yard also closed along with the signalbox. The station buildings were swept away and after being controlled by a ground frame between 1971 and 1979 the two sidings behind the down platform were also removed, leaving just a single line through the rationalised station, with a glorified bus shelter on the platform, making a forlorn sight compared with the thriving rail centre of yesteryear.

After leaving Penryn the line drops down through a deep cutting to Collegewood Viaduct. The viaduct achieved some degree of fame when in 1934 it became the very last Brunel/Brereton wooden-topped viaduct in the whole of Cornwall to be replaced, after 71 years of service. The viaduct was impressive, as is its successor, the original being 954ft long and 100ft high and built on a sweeping left hand curve with no fewer than 14 masonry piers. Again replacement was discussed as early as 1880 but it had timbers replaced over time and continued in service. The new all-masonry viaduct, built to the south of the original, was opened in July 1934 and even today it makes an impressive sight across the valley at Hillhead. Many of the old piers are still visible. Just over 1¼ miles beyond Collegewood Viaduct is Penmere, opened by the GWR as Penmere Platform on 1 June 1925. The small single-platform station was on a single line stretch until 1940 when four wartime War Department oil sidings on the up side were opened for military traffic. The sidings were linked to the main branch by a goods loop line that ran by the halt, also on the up side. In fact the sidings were not finally taken out of use until 1967, although they had been dormant for some time. In 1999 a new small brick shelter with a tiny awning replaced a primitive waiting hut. The line continues to descend at 1 in 80.

During 1970 somebody had the bright idea of opening a new Falmouth station that was more conveniently located for the town, compared with either Penmere or the 'old' Falmouth (Docks) stations. Initially called Falmouth, the new single-platform basic concrete structure opened on 7 December 1970 and Falmouth Docks station closed, even though the branch diesel unit continued to that site before reversing for the journey back to Truro. It is alleged that part of the concrete platform came from the 1963-closed Perranporth Beach Halt on the Chacewater to Newquay line. It was renamed 'The Dell' from 5 May 1975 when Falmouth Docks station reopened, rectifying the earlier nonsense. Finally this 1970 station was renamed again when, from 3 October 1988, it became Falmouth Town! The single line descends to Falmouth Docks, the end of the original CR railway and 312 miles and 49 chains from London via Bristol.

The original station here was impressive, with a main building that was 200ft long and 90ft wide, covered by an overall roof with a 70ft span. Every facility was provided for passengers and a large staff was employed to look after them. The station had two platform faces for passenger use, with a third road in the centre of the tracks for stock berthing. There was a substantial goods shed and yard on the up side with a crane, several sidings, a two-road locomotive shed with turntable and even a carriage turntable in the early days. On the down side were connections with the Falmouth docks complex, which possessed its own domestic fleet of shunting locomotives, steam giving way to diesel in the later years. The

track layout at the terminus changed many times but the greatest changes occurred in 1893, just after conversion from broad to standard gauge, and again in 1903. A new signalbox was erected in 1894, which survived until February 1966 when every piece of track at Falmouth Docks was removed, leaving just a single line stub of what had become a branch line and the rarely used connection with the docks lines, controlled by a ground frame. The overall roof had been removed in the late 1950s. Once upon a time there had been frequent through trains to London Paddington but over the years these gradually fizzled out, the last such trains running on Saturdays in the summer months, the very last being in September 1979 at the end of the summer season.

Falmouth Docks had grown over the years due largely to its prime position and its deep water availability. New dry docks were built and the town continues to have a buoyant ship repair business. The railway network within the docks complex was amazing with both main piers and just about every jetty and dry dock being rail served. The railway line to the docks opened on 14 January 1864, giving the Falmouth Docks Company direct access to the CR and the rest of the UK. There was a large foundry in the docks area and many auxiliary industries in the maritime field. There was great optimism about the future of the docks in Victorian times and indeed over the years various commodities were both imported and exported but never in the volume originally anticipated. In more recent times it was thought that a regular container flow might start and trials were conducted but to no avail. Calcified seaweed was also loaded at the docks but this was later undertaken in the goods yard at Truro. Fish traffic was another possibility and indeed in the distant past this was a regular source of income. However this payload did not survive the general purge of wagonload freight traffic that occurred during the 1960s, although a later trial was conducted. Reflecting this lack of freight traffic the docks railway network has now been abandoned and all the diminutive shunters have long disappeared but for strategic reasons the rail link between the branch and the docks is still in position, albeit heavily rusted.

The Cornish 'main line' label could realistically be applied to the Falmouth line only in mid- and late Victorian times. The combined populations of Redruth, Camborne and Penzance, plus the passenger traffic to and from the branches to Newquay (from Chacewater), Helston and St Ives, in addition to the Isles of Scilly, produced rail traffic patterns that tended to favour Penzance over Falmouth. There was also considerably more freight traffic from the far west, especially in the perishables, milk and postal categories, making the old WCR main line far more important. There is no doubt that by the time the broad gauge was abandoned in 1892 and tourism started to take off, Falmouth as a railway destination was decreasing in importance. For many decades the Falmouth line has had branch line status but having said that it was of sufficient importance to survive the 1960s purge of the Beeching era. In 2008 there were a dozen trains per day in each direction between Truro and Falmouth with a single diesel unit shuttling backwards and forwards all day, which compares favourably with 1863, when there were five round trips per day, while in 1927 there were 16. The current journey time for the 11¾-mile journey is a leisurely 23 minutes. Certainly the single line stub ending at Falmouth Docks is a sad sight compared with the frenetic scenes and remarkable infrastructure of a century ago; however in the spring of 2009, First Great Western and Network Rail collaborated in installing a passing track configuration at Penryn to increase line capacity and improve the service.

Left: **In this stirring view Carnon Viaduct across the tidal Restronguet Creek features prominently. This masonry viaduct was built in 1933 at a cost of £40,000, the replacement being built on the southern side of the original. The locomotive heading the return leg of the F&W Railtours 'Chopper Topper' railtour is No 37207, which proudly carries the 'Cornish Railways' insignia, applied during 1985/6 when Cornish railway management received limited operating autonomy. The special worked from Wolverhampton to Penzance via Falmouth on 8 June 1986. As viewed, Perranwell station is just beyond the distant end of the viaduct.** *Author*

Below: **With the hideous County Hall building in Truro as a backdrop, 'bubble' car No 55006 (shown as '106' on the cab front) leaves Cornwall's only city for Falmouth in March 1992. The 11-mile 29-chain journey from Penwithers Junction to Falmouth Docks is pleasant enough but the single-line branch hardly shapes up with the CR's grand plan for it to be the last section of the main line from Plymouth.** *Author*

Right: **This wonderful period view shows a GWR 4-4-0 stopping at Perranwell station with a down train in about 1900. At this time the station boasted a passing loop and a small goods yard but by far and away the most outstanding feature was the elevated signalbox that straddled a goods siding.** *Cornish Studies Library*

Middle: **This fine view of Perranwell station was taken when most of the infrastructure was intact. The up and down platforms were in use until 1966, when the up line was abandoned and later lifted. The unusual 21-lever elevated signalbox was closed at the same time, goods facilities having been withdrawn the previous year. For many years a camping coach was located in the sidings. The station became unstaffed in 1968.** *Author's Collection*

Below: **A typical branch train of the 1950s arrives at Perranwell's up platform behind immaculate small Prairie No 4588 in black livery, as a member of the station staff, with a centrally buttoned waistcoat, poses for the photographer. One of his duties will include 'whiting' the line on the edge of the coping stones on the platform's outer edge. Note the 305 mile post, representing the mileage from London via Bristol.** *David Lawrence*

Above: **Following the introduction of Class 165 'Network Turbos' on Paddington suburban lines during 1994 Network SouthEast two-car DMUs were decanted elsewhere, including Cornish branch lines. Here unit No L723 makes an incongruous sight as it leaves the 374yd Perran Tunnel with an up train in September 1994.**
Author

Below: **It is extremely difficult to find anything other than a diesel multiple-unit at work on the Falmouth branch and so the annual weed-killing run is high on the railway photographer's agenda. Passing the rationalised Perranwell station, which was devoid of its passing loop, buildings or signalbox, in April 1991, was the Chipmans train with Nos 20901 *Nancy* leading and No 20904 *Janis* trailing. The fine old goods shed survives in commercial use.**
Author

Above: The old Redruth & Chasewater Railway from Redruth and the mines around Gwennap down to the quay at Devoran was officially opened on 30 January 1826 and it was Cornwall's second railway of substance. Eventually horse traction gave way to steam locomotives. However, after the mining boom of the early 1860s traffic gradually declined and the old 4ft-gauge line ceased to operate from 25 September 1915. Here the old line passes beneath Carnon Viaduct on the Falmouth branch, which was a Margary Class A style, 756ft long and 96ft high. Some of the original piers survive to this day. *Cornish Studies Library*

Below: Few of the workforce in North America would have envisaged two of their high-tech, computer-controlled 3,300hp locomotives working on a Cornish single-track branch line with a Railhead Treatment train! The shine has been taken off Nos 66125 and 66038 by their duties as this rare locomotive-hauled working is about to enter Sparnock Tunnel on its way to Falmouth. *Sam Felce*

Above: **The Carnon Valley was once filled by silt brought downriver from the mines on higher ground towards Redruth. However, over the past century vegetation has gradually covered the deposits of mining activity, leaving few scars. With the gorse in bloom a two-car Class 150/2 heads for Truro from Falmouth in March 2007, watched by a lone dog walker.** *Author*

Below: **This photograph records an occasion that required an early start to the day. By the end of the summer of 1979 Falmouth was the penultimate branch line in Cornwall (the last being Newquay) to benefit from a through train to London on summer Saturdays and this was the penultimate weekend of operations before the service was axed forever. With Carnon Viaduct and the train looking magnificent in the early morning light, No 50044 *Exeter* heads its empty air-cons towards Falmouth for the 09.10 departure, on 22 September 1979. Note the old viaduct piers and the treacherous mud in the foreground.** *Author*

Right: **This photographic gem was found deep in the RIC archive in Truro. It shows a very early Victorian scene from the days of the broad gauge at Penryn station. The railway opened in 1863 and outside the original CR building are local children, railway employees and workers plus a horse-drawn omnibus, with top-hatted gentlemen perched beside the driver. The station was replaced in 1923, when a new station opened on a slightly relocated site.** *Royal Institution of Cornwall*

Middle: **The same original building featured above can be seen here on the right as a down mid-morning train arrives at Penryn in Edwardian times. Penryn was an important railhead at the turn of the 20th century not only because of the town's 3,000 population but because the large goods yard was a focal point for farmers from miles around. There seems to be two or three coaches behind the 4-4-0 locomotive.** *Author's Collection*

The Station, Penryn

Below: **Historically this is a most interesting picture of Penryn because it shows both the new post-1923 station building and platforms on the left and the original CR station on the right (look for the two tall light-coloured chimneys to the left of the goods shed). This shows precisely the extent of the station relocation. Looking towards Truro, probably in the late 1940s, the view also shows the extent of the goods yard, with sidings at both the up and down ends of the down side platform.** *P. Q. Treloar Collection*

Left: **Who would ever have imagined that the railway complex featured opposite, with its entire wonderful infrastructure, could have been so desecrated in the space of just 50 years? In this rather depressing photograph from September 2008, FGW No 150244, strengthened by the addition of a Class 153 for crowds visiting Falmouth to see the tall ships, passes the small waiting hut on the single platform at Penryn with just a single track with no sidings in evidence. In May 2009 a revised track layout at Penryn would allow branch trains to pass, thereby increasing line capacity.** *Author*

Below: **By September 2005 the old up platform was completely covered in foliage, giving the impression of a very cramped site. A small tasteful brick-built shelter with compact awning has been provided but the days of a roaring fire in the waiting room have gone forever. Arriving in pouring rain is a Truro-bound single-car unit in the shape of No 153382, which is in black and gold livery.** *Author*

Above: Although this classic photograph has been published previously it does illustrate an important moment in Cornish railway history, the abolition of the very last Brunel/Brereton/Margary wooden-topped viaduct. The scene is Collegewood Viaduct, south of Penryn, and the new masonry structure can be seen on the left with a two-coach branch train heading for Falmouth Docks. A total of 18 railway workmen are posing beside a trolley on the old 954ft-long, 100ft-high Margary Class A viaduct. The old viaduct lasted from 1863 until 1934, a total of 71 years. *Royal Institution of Cornwall*

Below: **On 31 October 1898 the 5.20pm mixed 'Mail' train headed by 0-4-4T No 3542 derailed on the embankment south of Collegewood Viaduct, tearing up a length of track in the process. The locomotive and leading coach crashed down the slope but only the leading mail coach turned completely on its side. Unfortunately Driver Cotterill died of scalding but happily none of the passengers perished in what became known as the 'Hill Head disaster'.** *Cornish Studies Library*

Left: The next two stations between Penryn and Falmouth Docks are Penmere and Falmouth Town. Opened on 1 June 1925 as Penmere Platform, the single platform station serves the outskirts of Falmouth. Nowadays known as simply Penmere, all of the buildings seen in this 1950s view have since been demolished. The weed-covered track in the foreground led to four World War 2 War Department oil sidings that were finally disconnected in 1967. *Author's Collection*

Below: Proving that Penmere makes its contribution to the Falmouth branch line income is this April 1991 shot of DMU P874 arriving with a Truro-bound train as 11 passengers emerge from a squalid hut. This has since been replaced by a basic but stylish brick structure with an attractive awning. In the background to the right can be seen the space once occupied by the four War Department oil sidings. *Author*

Right: **Three-car suburban DMU No P319 enters the cutting at the north end of Collegewood Viaduct (which can just be seen) with a Falmouth Docks to Truro working on 1 July 1981. Various classes of diesel mechanical unit worked the Falmouth branch for more than 30 years, exceeded in longevity only by the '45xx' class 2-6-2 prairie tanks.** *Author*

Below: **This pristine Class 45xx Prairie tank engine makes a vigorous start from Falmouth Docks with a Truro train that comprises a six-wheeler in a bogie coach sandwich. The two-road engine shed on the right was closed from 21 September 1925 but the 41-lever signalbox far left lasted from 1894 until 1966, when the Falmouth end of the branch was reduced to a single-line stub.**
P. Q. Treloar Collection

Left: **Although not technically perfect, this rare 1870 view of a CR mail train on an embankment just outside of Falmouth Docks station, has been published previously. The locomotive has been identified as ex-SDR broad-gauge 4-4-0ST *Mazeppa*, built in 1859 by Slaughter & Gruning of Bristol. The leading vehicle is a mail coach followed by a second class coach with luggage space on top. Note the disc and crossbar signal.** *Cornish Studies Library*

Middle: **This scene shows a notable event, the last visit to the Falmouth branch by 'Western' Class 52s in the days of British Railways. On 4 December 1976 the author organised the 'Western China Clay' tour that had run down from Paddington overnight. No D1056 *Western Sultan* is seen at Falmouth Docks awaiting departure for Truro. At the other end of the train was No D1023 *Western Fusilier*. The train went on to visit Newquay and Carne Point, Fowey. The 'Westerns' were finally withdrawn in February 1977.** *Author*

Below: **This branch train has just left Falmouth Town station, which opened on 7 December 1970. The station was originally called Falmouth but in 1975 it was renamed The Dell, before being renamed Falmouth Town from 3 October 1988. Working the branch in September 1994 was this Network SouthEast-liveried two-car DMU. In the background is the tidal harbour at Penryn.** *Author*

Right: **This scene depicts the first CR broad gauge train to arrive at the Falmouth terminus on 24 August 1863. Note all of the civil dignitaries in the left foreground. The locomotive has been suitably decorated for the occasion.** *Brunel University*

Left: **The author rescued this remarkable item from a house clearance via eBay, the original being a faded framed print in its 'as delivered' but damaged frame. The photograph shows the staff at Falmouth Docks station in about 1890, because the tracks in the background are clearly broad gauge. The various hats have GWR embroidered on them and while no names are available it is possible to determine grade by headgear and the size of the watch fobs!** *Author's Collection*

Right: **These exceptionally unusual visitors to Falmouth Docks rolled into town on 22 March 1992. Working the 07.15 Basingstoke to Falmouth and Newquay, alias Merlin Railtours 'Cornish Construction Crompton', were Nos 33050 *Isle of Grain* and No 33063. Class 37 No 37675 was at the other end of the train, there being no run round facilities at Falmouth Docks.** *Author*

Above: **Although the long corrugated roof awning at Falmouth Docks has survived, the rest of the site shows almost total dereliction. The disused lines down to the docks can just be seen to the left of single power car No 109, which is arriving from Truro in August 1988. The town of Falmouth can be seen in the background.** *Author*

Middle: **Strange to relate that although Falmouth Docks station is now in very poor condition the growth of weeds and shrubs makes the scene aesthetically attractive, like some remote and long-lost branch line. Pausing in the sunshine against the buffer stops is Network SouthEast liveried two-car No L723, while in the background there remains a little evidence of the nearby presence of the docks.** *Author*

Left: **Although over the years Falmouth Docks has developed as a ship refurbishment and repair centre, in recent times there has never been a sustained source of freight by rail originating in the docks. There have been numerous experiments and short-term loads have included fish, fertiliser, domestic coal containers and Freightliner traffic but they have all come to nothing. The link to the docks can be seen on the left as DMU P109 leaves Falmouth Docks with the 11.58 departure in October 1988.** *Author*

Right: **The long awning on the left of this late 1950s photograph of Falmouth Docks terminus is all that remains in 2009. The overall roof seems to have been demolished in the early 1960s. The other lines, platforms and loading docks were abolished years ago as rationalisation became the order of the day. The vital statistics of the original building were impressive, it being 200ft long, 90ft wide with an all-over roof span of 70 feet.**
Cornish Studies Library

Middle: **This view shows Falmouth Docks at its worst in August 1992, with one of the utility Class 150/2 units pausing at the sole surviving platform on a filthy day weather-wise. All the fine buildings of yesteryear have been razed but with the addition of a 'Portacabin'! At least there are no staffing costs and, once the awning falls down, there will be no building maintenance – hardly the grand vision of the CR in its Acts of 1846 and 1861!**
Author

Below: **This photograph records the visit to Falmouth Docks of a famous locomotive, No 3440 *City of Truro*, on 14 February 1961 when it was hired by Westward Television to haul the 'Westward Television Exhibition Train'. The 4-4-0 is alleged to have been the first locomotive to have exceeded 100mph on the GWR in 1904. It was saved from the scrapheap and preserved for posterity.**
Westward Television

Above: Until the spring of 2009, the line from Penwithers Junction, Truro to Falmouth Docks comprised just a single track throughout without any passing loops or sidings, except for the weed-covered connection down to Falmouth Docks, seen here in 1992. However, to the surprise of many, First Great Western and Network Rail collaborated to install a passing line at Penryn with the objective of increasing services on the CR's former 'main line'. *Author*

Below: **This aerial shot of Falmouth shows the headland occupied by Pendennis Castle, nearest the camera. Sheltered behind the headland is Falmouth Docks and to the right Carrick Roads. Falmouth Docks station can just be detected in the centre of this general view of the area.** *Author's Collection*

Plymouth, Saltash, Liskeard, Bodmin, Lostwithiel, St. Austell, Truro, and Penzance.—Cornwall & West Cornwall.
Sec., W. H. Bond.—*Cornwall.*   Sec. and Supt., C. P. Carlton. Penzance : Assistant Sec., G. S. Denbigh.—*West Cornwall.*

(Bradshaws timetable, April 1861 — Cornwall and West Cornwall. Down and Up trains, Week Days and Sundays, with fares in 1st, 2nd and 3rd class. Stations include London, Bristol, Exeter, St. David's St., Plymouth, Devonport, Saltash, St. Germans, Menheniot, Liskeard, Doublebois, Bodmin R., Lostwithiel, Par, St. Austell, Grampound Rd, Truro, Flmth 'busa, Chacewater, Scorrier Gate, Redruth, Pool, Camborne, Gwinear Road, Hayle, St. Ives Road, Marazion Road, Penzance, Perranwell, Penryn, Falmouth.)

This remarkable timetable from Bradshaws dated April 1861 features the Cornish main line, with the Cornwall Railway's broad-gauge trains running from Plymouth Millbay to Truro and the West Cornwall Railway's standard-gauge trains from Truro to Penzance. The railway line to Falmouth was not opened until 1863. Passengers on the 9.15am from Paddington would be in Penzance by 9.5pm the same day! Passengers should change at Redruth for Falmouth, Camborne for Helston and Hayle for St Ives.

Plymouth (Millby) d	4 40	6 50	9 20	11 0	....	....	2 40	....	5 0	....	6 6	6 45	8 10	....	11 5
Devonport ....[ton		6 57	9 26	11 7	....	....	2 47	....	5 7	....	6 10	6 51	8 19	....	1110
Saltash, for Calling-	4 51	7 5	9 34	1116	....	....	2 56	....	5 16	....		6 58	8 27	....	1120
St. Germans		7 18	9 46	1128	....	....	3 8	....	5 29	....	a	7 8	8 40		
Menheniot, for Looe		7 32		1142	....	....	3 22	....	5 43	....			8 52		
Liskeard	5 20	7 42	10 6	1152	....	....	3 33	....	5 53	....	6 41		9 1		
Doublebois		7 52		12 2	....	....	3 43	....	6 3						
Bodmin Road †17..	5 38	8 7	1025	1217	....	....	3 55	....	6 16	....	7 1				
Lostwithiel [Ln p14]		8 17	1033	1227	....	....	4 5	....	6 25						
Par (Cornwall Min.		8 31	....	1239	....	....	4 17	....	6 39	....	7 17				
St. Austell	6 2	8 44	1053	1252	....	....	4 30	....	6 52	....	7 29				
Burngullow		8 50		1258	....	....	4 36	....	6 58						
Grampound Road		9 1		1 9	....	....	4 47	....	7 9						
Truro .... arr	6 29	9 18	1122	1 26	....	aft	5 3	aft	7 27	....	7 54				
Falmouth Branch Truro......dep	6 40	9 32	1132	1 33	....	3 37	5 15	6 5	8 5	....	8 5				
Perranwell		9 42	1142	1 47	....	3 46	5 25	6 15	8 15		8 15				
Penryn, frHlstn	6 54	9 52	1152	1 57	....	3 55	5 35	6 25	8 25		8 25				
Falmouth ..arr	7 2	10 1	12 2	2 7	....	4 5	5 45	6 35	8 35		8 35				
Truro......dep	6 35	9 25	1129	1 32		5 8	Stop	7 33	8 0						
Chacewater		9 38	....	1 45		5 21		7 45							
Scorrier Gate		9 44	....	1 51		5 27	aft	7 51							
Redruth	6 55	9 52	1154	1 59	....	5 35	5 45	7 59	8 20						
Carn Brea		9 58	1159	2 5	....	5 40	5 50	8 5							
Camborne	7 5	10 5	12 5	2 12	....	5 47	5 56	8 11	8 28						
Gwinear Road 15		1012	1214	2 19	....	5 54	6 2	8 17	8 35						
Hayle..[see page 15.]		1023	1222	2 29	....	6 4	....	8 26	8 42						
St. Erth (For St. Ives	7 23	1028	1228	2 35	....	6 10	....	8 32	8 47						
Marazion Road		1033	1237	2 44	....	6 20	....	8 40	8 55						
Penzance.........arr	7 35	1045	1242	2 50	....	6 25	....	8 45	9 0						

The weekday timetable for down trains on the Cornish main line from the November 1888 issue of Bradshaws. Note the names of the intermediate stations and the fact that even 120 years ago the Falmouth line was clearly referred to as the 'Falmouth Branch'.

Up.	mrn	1&2	mrn	gov	gov	gov	mrn	1&2	aft	gov	aft	aft	aft	aft	aft	gov	aft
Penzance ....dep	....		....	6 25			10 0	1115			2 5	....	5 0	6 35			
Marazion Road.........			....	6 31			10 6	1120			2 11	....		6 41			
St. Erth (For St. Ives,			....	6 40			1015	1129			2 21	....	5 11	6 52			
Hayle....[see page 15.)			....	6 46			1021	....			2 27			6 58			
Gwinear Road 15			....	6 56			1032	....			2 38	5 5		7 9			
Camborne.............			....	7 4			1040	1146			2 46	5 12	....	7 17			
Carn Brea			....	7 10			1046	....			2 52	5 18		7 23			
Redruth..............			....	7 16			1053	1157			3 0	5 23	5 34	7 30			
Scorrier Gate			....	7 23			11 0	....			3 8			7 37			
Chacewater			....	7 29			11 6	....			3 14	Stop		7 45			
Truro 18 ....arr			....	7 41			1118	1217			3 26	aft	5 53	7 57			
Mls Falmouth ....dep			....	7 8	8 45	1045	1140				2 50	4 30	5 25	6 55			
3¼ Penryn, for Helston			....	7 18	8 55	1055	1151				3 0	4 40	5 34	7 5			
7¼ Perranwell			....	7 28	9 5	11 5	12 1				3 10	4 50		7 15			
11¼ Truro 18......arr			....	7 38	9 15	1115	1211				3 20	5 0	5 51	7 25			
Truro ....dep			....	7 48			1128	1223			3 33	Stop	6 8	6 55			
Grampound Road......			....	8 5			1145	....			3 50			8 22			
Burngullow..........			....	8 15			1156	....			4 0	....		8 32			
St. Austell [Line, p.14.)			....	8 22			12 3	1251			4 8		6 30	8 39			
Par (Cornwall Minerals			....	8 32			1214	....			4 18		6 40	8 49			
Lostwithiel			....	8 45			1226	....			4 30		6 52	9 1			
Bodmin Road * 17....			....	8 55			1235	1 12			4 39	....	7 2	9 10			
Doublebois..........			....	9 12			1251	....			4 56			9 26			
Liskeard.............			7 23	9 23			1 1	1 31			5 6		7 25	9 36			
Menheniot, for Looe ..			7 31	9 32			1 10	....			5 15	aft		9 45			
St. Germans..........			7 43	9 45			1 22	....			5 30	7 25		9 57			
Saltash, for Callington			7 56	9 58			1 34	....			5 44	7 37	7 53	10 9			1125
Devonport			8 5	10 8			1 43	2 2			5 53	7 46	8 1	1017			1133
Plymouth (Millbay) arr			8 12	1018			1 50	2a6			6 5	7 55	8 10	1026			1140

(Side notes: "adelridge, Padstow, Camelford, and Boscastle. Per Steamer from Company's Pier." — "& North Road Station." — "6 48, and 8 18 aft. ney, 7 minutes." — "run for Passengers proceeding to Paignton and Stations ping Carriage (1st class) from Plymouth to London." — "Wednesdays and Saturdays.")

Truro to Falmouth Docks

Mondays to Fridays

Operator	GW	GW	GW	GW	GW	GW	GW	GW	GW	GW	GW	GW
Notes & Facilities												
Plymouth **d**			0705	0919	0923	1117	1310	1511	1557		1840	1950
Penzance **d**	0542	0643	0743	0845	1000	1140	1242	1450	1644	1735	1905	2011
‡ Truro **d**	0631	0731	0832	0945	1047	1239	1429	1628	1726	1822	2000	2104
Perranwell **d**	0638	0738	0839	0952	1054	1246	1436	1635	1733	1829	2007	2111
Penryn **d**	0645	0745	0845	0959	1101	1253	1443	1641	1739	1835	2014	2118
Penmere **d**	0649	0749	0849	1003	1105	1257	1447	1645	1743	1839	2018	2122
Falmouth Town **d**	0651	0751	0851	1005	1107	1259	1449	1647	1745	1841	2020	2124
Falmouth Docks **a**	0654	0754	0854	1008	1110	1302	1452	1650	1748	1844	2023	2127
Falmouth Docks **d**	0657	0757	0857	1011	1147	1327	1457	1653	1751	1912	2026	2130
Falmouth Town **d**	0659	0759	0859	1013	1149	1329	1459	1655	1753	1914	2028	2132
Penmere **d**	0702	0802	0902	1016	1152	1332	1502	1658	1756	1917	2031	2135
Penryn **d**	0707	0807	0906	1021	1157	1337	1507	1703	1800	1921	2036	2140
Perranwell **d**	0714	0814	0913	1028	1204	1344	1514	1710	1807	1928	2043	2147
‡ Truro **a**	0721	0821	0920	1035	1211	1351	1521	1717	1814	1935	2050	2154
Penzance **a**	0827b	0914	1019	1124	1321	1441	1636	1806	1937	2041	2147	2310
Plymouth **a**	0851	0945	1039	1157	1332	1555	1655	1841	1933	2109	2216	0007

Truro to Falmouth Docks

Saturdays

Operator	GW	GW	GW	GW	GW	GW	GW	GW	GW	GW	GW	GW
Notes & Facilities												
Plymouth **d**		0550		0813	1000	1123	1310	1441	1511		1840	1950
Penzance **d**	0530	0604	0743	0848	1036	1145		1450	1554	1640	1908	
‡ Truro **d**	0625	0730	0830	0943	1125	1247	1435	1558	1651	1802	1956	2104
Perranwell **d**	0632	0737	0837	0950	1132	1254	1442	1605	1658	1809	2003	2111
Penryn **d**	0639	0744	0844	0957	1139	1301	1449	1612	1705	1816	2010	2118
Penmere **d**	0643	0748	0848	1001	1143	1305	1453	1616	1709	1820	2014	2122
Falmouth Town **d**	0645	0750	0850	1003	1145	1307	1455	1618	1711	1822	2016	2124
Falmouth Docks **a**	0648	0753	0853	1006	1148	1310	1458	1621	1714	1825	2019	2127
Falmouth Docks **d**	0653	0756	0856	1009	1151	1313	1501	1624	1725	1828	2026	2131
Falmouth Town **d**	0655	0758	0858	1011	1153	1315	1503	1626	1727	1830	2028	2133
Penmere **d**	0658	0801	0901	1014	1156	1318	1506	1629	1730	1833	2031	2136
Penryn **d**	0703	0806	0906	1019	1201	1323	1511	1634	1735	1838	2036	2141
Perranwell **d**	0710	0813	0913	1026	1208	1330	1518	1641	1742	1845	2043	2148
‡ Truro **a**	0717	0820	0920	1033	1215	1337	1525	1648		1852	2050	2155
Penzance **a**	0827		1015	1126	1323	1446	1636	1757	1923	1949	2143	2317
Plymouth **a**	0844	0948	1043	1157	1338	1555	1700	1839		2112	2240	

Above: **The up train weekday timetable for November 1888. Note that passengers should change for the Cornwall Minerals Railway at Par (the Newquay branch), Menheniot for Looe and Saltash for Callington, the last two connecting with coach services.**

Left: **The Falmouth branch timetable from April 2008. From May 2009 a passing facility at Penryn will allow for an even more comprehensive service on the well-patronised 146-year-old branch line.**

Appendix 2

Gradient Profile and Routes

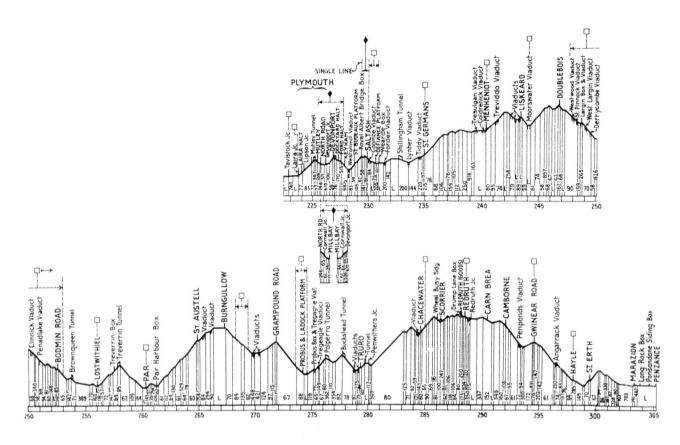

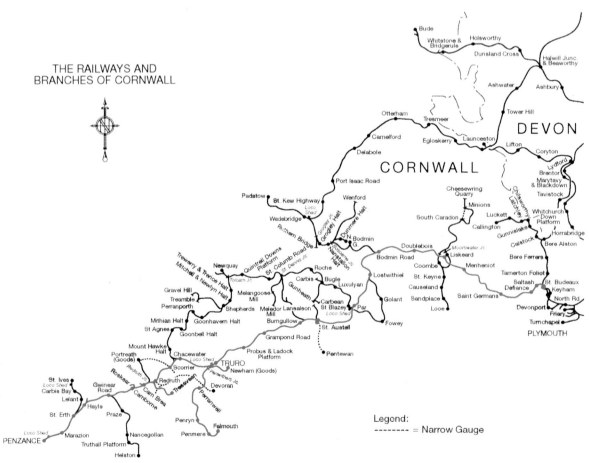

THE RAILWAYS AND
BRANCHES OF CORNWALL

Legend:
-------- = Narrow Gauge

Index by Chapter